Poor Patrick's Proverbs, Poems, Pontifications & Quotations

Poor Patrick's Proverbs, Poems, Pontifications & Quotations

VOLUME 1

PATRICK E. TRUJILLO

Published by Patrick Ernesto Trujillo, North Bergen, New Jersey
poorpatricksprovs.net

Cover design: Kerrie Robertson
Cover photograph: Robert Ferrer of Ferrer Photo Studio

ISBN: 9780692571002
e-ISBN: 9780692571019

Printed in the United States of America

To my
beloved wife Ilia,
whose inspiration and help
made this book possible.

CONTENTS

Introduction 1

   Chapter One: Celibacy 3

   Chapter Two: Institution 13

   Chapter Three: Marriage 23

   Chapter Four: Married Priests 27

   Chapter Five: Miscellaneous 35

   Chapter Six: Morality 45

   Chapter Seven: Poetry 73

   Chapter Eight: Politics 115

   Chapter Nine: Prayer 119

   Chapter Ten: Proverbs 159

   Chapter Eleven: Songs/Music 275

   Chapter Twelve: Writing 281

Bibliography 291

Acknowledgments 295

About the Author 297

INTRODUCTION

Poor Patrick's Proverbs, Poems, Pontifications & Quotations,
volume 1 springs from homespun philosophy and an admiration for Benjamin Franklin's *Poor Richard's Almanack* and
John Bartlett's *Familiar Quotations*, interspersed with a serious study of history.

Young adults, seminarians, and university and college
students will find inspiration in evaluating the twelve topics
presented. These themes, catalysts for discussion, meditation, further elucidation, and action serve as the rationale
for writing this book. Married priests will see celibacy, for
example, for the shell that it is and marriage as a time-honored fulfillment.

Others will note the distinct difference, the sharp contrast, between institution and church. Encapsulated in pithy
dictums are morality and politics, while poetry, prayer, proverbs, and songs and music stand on their own merit like gold
nuggets of contemplation.

In conclusion, tongue-in-cheek satire, miscellaneous
parody, and exaggeration find their place in Patrick's pontifications, while writing is presented as the precisely powerful
instrument that it is.

CHAPTER ONE

CELIBACY

1. **CELIBACY HARVEST**

   Sexual immorality is an offshoot of the Papal Ban on Priestly Marriage, dating back to 1095, when it was issued.

2. **CELIBACY'S CHARISM**

   C = Christian

   H = Hellish

   A = Active

   R = Repugnant

   I = Institutionalized

   S = Sexually active

   M = Mechanistic

3. **ILLUSORY CELIBACY**

   Are numerous celibates immoral, amoral *castrati* in an institution's alluring, illusory song of innocence?

4. **(HOLY) ORDER**

   Celibacy is greater than marriage, and obedience is the greatest virtue of all—for some folks.

5. **STUCK**

   Many a mitred man is mired in the muck of misogyny, mismanagement, and mayhem.

6. **STANDARD**

   If corrupt vowed celibates are the standards of perfection, then rot runs rampant in Rio.

7. **CONTRADICTIONS**

   If one is going to get laicized, he might as well get "unbaptized" and "unconfirmed," too. Contradictions never cease.

8. **VOWED CELIBACY 101**

   . . . is a public relations ploy.

9. **FUNCTIONARIES**

   Celibacy makes too many infamous functionary flunkies in a defunct institution.

10. **VOWED CELIBACY?**

    Is vowed celibacy a mockery of marriage?

11. **VOWED CELIBACY**

    Is vowed celibacy a front for continual corruption, scriptural and historical errors, and worse?

12. **PHARAOH**

The modern-day pharaoh wears white and obstinately refuses to free his charges from the moral, psychological shackles of vowed celibacy.

13. **DECEIT**

The vow of priestly celibacy is a fraudulent contract because those responsible for receiving the vows of celibacy have not adequately explained the true history of celibacy to those who have taken those vows.

14. **PELAGIANISM AND CELIBACY**

Pelagianism finds its expression in vowed celibacy.

15. **PROMISCUITY**

Celibacy is a loophole for promiscuous sex.

16. **CELIBACY PAR EXCELLENCE**

Where is the primacy, value, and charism of celibacy in the life of Pope Alexander VI (Rodrigo Borgia), who fathered three children while he was cardinal and six more after he became pope?
(See Sarah Bradford, *Lucrezia Borgia*, pp. xvi–xvii.)

17. **"GRACED" POSITION**
Vowed celibacy is nothing more than peligianism posing as a "graced" position.

18. **DOUBLE EVIL**
Does vowed celibacy disgrace sex and dishonor marriage?

19. **HALLMARKS**
Suppression, repression, oppression, and depression seem to be hallmarks of the totalitarian vowed celibate state.

20. **LOVE CHILD**
Vowed celibacy is the love child of Manichaeanism and Stoicism.

21. **PLAYBOY CELIBATE PRIEST**
The Bishop of Liège, Belgium, who lived in the twelfth and thirteenth centuries had sixty-five illegitimate children and seventy concubines, some of whom were nuns and one of whom was a Benedictine abbess.
(See Nigel Cawthorne, *Sex Lives of the Popes*, p. 11)

22. CONDITIONAL LOVE

Too many celibates seem to live the dictum "Lie with, lie to, love 'em and leave 'em."

23. SINPROOF

Is celibacy a sinproof suit?

24. CRUCIFIXION

Too many children are crucified daily by the lack of love of their callous celibate priest fathers.

25. BISHOPACCOUNTABILITY.ORG

More than 3,700 celibate priests are listed, along with allegations of sexual abuse against these individuals from newspapers and others sources.

26. THE LAW OF CELIBACY

The Law of Celibacy is indefensible, fallible, and inflammatory. Does it promote unity, growth, and harmony?

27. PREFERENCE

Celibacy can lead to fear, fault, failure, and frustration, while marriage involves fulfillment, fairness, forgiveness, and faith.

28. HOW MANY?

How many are children, grandchildren, great-grandchildren, and great-great-grandchildren of celibate priests?

29. SLAVERY FORM

Vowed celibacy manipulates a man's mind, coerces his conscience, and strangles his soul with the invisible nylon cord of lies, half-truths, and powerful propaganda.

30. CELIBACY'S FRUITION

Celibacy's fruit is seen in newspapers, in other media, and in multiple court records in the United States and in at least twenty-six other countries.

31. PROGENY ENCOUNTER

Is the reason so few celibate priests work with gangs because they fear they might one day meet their own progeny?

32. CHAOTIC CAREER

The "chaos," which celibate clergy ascribe to married priests, is clearly seen in the faces of celibates themselves.

33. **HUSH-HUSH**

A man can have a lover or two or more, sire a child or many children, but as long as he keeps this "hush-hush," the man is still considered celibate. He has kept his holy vow not to marry. Hmmm . . . Shame.

34. **CELEBRATION?**

Some celebrate their state of celibacy—when they sleep.

35. **G3**

Celibacy, the "golden goose of greed," serves avarice and control very well.

36. **SMELL**

When celibacy trumps the need and vision of the people, then the stench of parochialism pervades the air.

37. **PLUS & MINUS**

Optional celibacy counts multiple achievements while imposed celibacy numbers more than 3,700 celibate priests in BishopAccountability.org in the US alone.

38. **PITY**

If celibacy is the standard for humanity, pity humanity.

39. **CAVEAT/BEWARE**

The vow of celibacy does not guarantee chastity nor control of the sex drive.

40. **NO GUARANTEE**

Celibacy does not protect one from promiscuity.

41. **DISPENSABLE FUNCTIONARIES**

Are celibate priests pawns in an institution's (em)ploy?

CHAPTER TWO

INSTITUTION

42. **DOUBLE DANGER**

Hiding pedophile clergy harkens back to the hiding of important historical facts.

43. **WAR MONGERING**

Did the Fourth Lateran Council cover up the crimes of the Fifth Crusade with religious mandates?

44. **SINLESS**

Certain clergy must be without sin (immaculate like the doctrine they espouse) since they cast excommunication stones at those who do not belong to the same "club."

45. **DECEPTION**

Denying and hiding rather than transparency and openness have become normative for many.

46. **SUBSTITUTES**

If power, money, and deception have replaced faith, hope, and charity, then the former have become the gods of many.

47. **SHADE (HA-HAH-SAH-RAH)**

. . . is Refuge from ultraconservativism's rays, which cause apostolic paralysis and egoism's contagion.

48. **CAVEAT QUIP**

Layperson, if you wear your woolen winter scarf like a stole, you may be excommunicated by those in authority for impersonating a priest.

49. **INFALLIBILITY SYNDROME**

Because a person holds a position of authority, that does not necessarily make him right.

50. **PROTOCOL**

If some folks can call degenerate celibates "Father," then they shouldn't have any qualms about calling a married priest "Father."

51. **SAINT SUBSTITUTE**

Will St. Dismas, the Good Thief, be replaced by another canonized "saint"?

52. **JUSTICE?**

When pedophile priests are sentenced to a life of prayer and penance, then all of us are as innocent or guilty as they.

53. **SIN LIVER**

According to some, a married priest is living in sin with the woman of his dreams while certain clergy are living the perfect celibate state.

54. **INERRANCY**

Inerrancy is a complex invention used to justify the raw abuse of power.

55. **INFALLIBLE DEEDS**

. . . are as "extremely complex" as the foundation used to support them.

56. **OLD CATHOLIC**

Being Old Catholic liberates one from Rome's rules.

57. **HIGH-STAKES SCANDALS**

When an institution can get away with murder, narcotics dealing, theft, fraud, and embezzlement, then hiding pedophiles is just another pawn in the play.

58. **OF A FEATHER**

Totalitarian governments and institutions love to window-dress and maintain a constant barrage of disinformation.

59. **SERVANT CHURCH**

Being servant encapsulates community, sacrament, herald or proclaimer of the good news, and institution insofar as institution embodies the first three.

60. **DEFIANCE AND REVENGE**

With the living and even with the dead, certain institutions continue to show defiance and seek revenge.

61. **MONOPOLY**

Certain institutions have monopolies on their buildings, property, and assets, but not on their people.

62. **CHOKE HOLD**

Those in authority sometimes try to extend their ugly, choking tentacles into every aspect of religious life.

63. **TENTACLES OF DEATH**

Certain CEOs, immune from punishment for wrongdoing, seem quite quick to criticize, ostracize, and demonize religious women who do tremendous good.

64. **DISTRACTION**

For a certain institution to focus on nuns' "wayward ways" is to lose sight of its own serious violations.

65. **BLAME SHIFTING**

How can an institution accuse others of wrongdoing when it is riddled with corruption?

66. **MUSCLES**

There are those who love to flex their muscles in the presence of those weaker than them.

67. **GROWTH**

At the rate the institution is going, the *excommunicandi* (the excommunicated) will soon outnumber "the faithful."

68. CLIPPED WINGS

If we can't clip the money wing$ of certain institutions, then we will clip their wings of verbosity and prevarication.

69. CALUMNY/SLANDER

Defamation, derision, and derogatory remarks are part of the *modus procedendi* and *modus vivendi* of the religious elite.

70. SELFISHNESS

Some who take a vow of poverty show a powerful propensity to selfishness.

71. FAÇADE

Within magnificent buildings hide heinous crimes, serious omissions, and dastardly deviations of every kind.

72. THREE-HEADED VIPER

Certain institutions have the following characteristics: religiosity on the outside and viciousness, vindictiveness, and revenge on the inside.

73. **INSTITUTION VERSUS CHURCH**

The Church is collegial, while an institution is hierarchical.

CHAPTER THREE

MARRIAGE

74. **MARRIAGE**

Marriage is a commitment of love, care, concern, and respect.

75. **SPOUSAL ADVICE**

Let's not kiss too long, or our passions will go out of control.

76. **VITAMIN D3**

One's spouse is like vitamin D3, the daily sunshine of one's home.

77. **UNRAVEL**

Unraveling the knot in one's spouse's fine silver chain necklace is as important as anything else one can do.

78. **HOLY OBEDIENCE**

Parents are on call 24/7 to the cry, clamor, and call of their newborn baby.

79. **REMEDY**

When your spouse endures intense pain, you must lavish them with playful compliments, assurances, and adulations of their physical beauty and prowess and be the cool clown in their closet of consternation.

80. **MULTISENSORY**

Does one's spouse have the olfactory sense greater than that of a grizzly bear, the eye of an eagle, and the combined supersensitivity of St. Bridget of Kildaire and St. Catherine of Sienna?

81. **DELIGHT**

The presence of one's spouse is better than ripe mangos—ready to be plucked, sucked, sipped, and savored to the core.

82. **CONNUBIAL BLISS**

Wisdom and humor are a well-wedded wonder.

83. **SEXUALITY/SPIRITUALITY**

Is there a difference between sexuality and spirituality?

84. **BOTTOM LINE**

In a marriage commitment, the bottom line, the most important line, is "I love you."

85. **REALLY?**

When one's spouse gets superserious, lighten the load, get funny, and make them laugh.

CHAPTER FOUR

MARRIED PRIESTS

86. **DISCIPLINED LOOK**

The wild, wintry Wyoming wind blows across the New Jersey shore and messes up many a spouse's coiffure.

87. **RAISON D'AMOUR**

Whose wife loves him for his costly yarmulke, his invaluable tallit, and his worn-out socks?

88. **JEALOUSY**

Who doesn't become jealous of his wife's cellular phone when she puts it in her bra?

89. **PARADOX**

One's wife's wild, disciplined look leaves her enchanted, distinctly elegant, and unique.

90. **ABRAHAM'S PROGENY**

Even in old age, spiritual children continue to be born to a married priest and his spouse.

91. **UNION**

. . . is stronger than celibacy.

92. **JUSTICE'S PRICE**

The character of many married priests has been
flogged, brutally torn away, and maligned for centuries.
Conscience wounds are left to fester, become infected
and purulent. Only common criminals are so despised.

93. **MODERN-DAY MARTYRDOM**

Many married priests have been derided, humiliated,
berated, belittled, and psychologically brutalized. No
small wonder they want nothing to do with official
ministry.

94. **WITNESSES**

Married priests fulfill Genesis 2:18 and 2:23. ("It is not
good that man should be alone; I will make [him] a
helper. . . . This is now bone of my bones and flesh of my
flesh.")

95. **TESTIMONY**

Married priests bear testimony to the ancient blessing,
creativity, and fulfillment of marriage.

96. **CONJOINED TWINS**

A married priest and his wife are spiritual conjoined
twins.

97. CLERGY CRIMINALS

If married priests are criminals, then those that condemned Galileo and other innocent victims are far worse.

98. ST. JOVINIAN, PATRON OF MARRIED PRIESTS

Jovinian, "arrested and beaten with leaded scourges, then to be exiled" by Emperor Maximus, who was a friend of Bishop Ambrose, a former Roman general, is hailed by the author of this book as the Martyr Saint of Married Priests.

(See Samuel Eliot, *History of Liberty*, volume 2, p. 17)

99. POPE VERSUS GENESIS

In 385, Pope Siricius decreed that priests may no longer sleep with their wives.

(See "A Brief History of Celibacy in the Catholic Church")

100. IRONY

Married priests have charmed the world, and the institution punishes them. (Adapted from the eleventh line of Francois Voltaire's "La Morte de Mademoiselle Lecouvreur": "*Elle a charmé le monde, et vous l'en punissez.*")

(See Will & Ariel Durant, *The Age of Voltaire*, p. 32)

101. BETTER CHOICE

Being a married priest is better than being promiscuous.

102. SECRET LANGUAGE

"Cuandi coux-coux chi letani," I tenderly tell my wife in our secretly created language, which means, "My beautiful multicolored blossom atop a seventy-eight-foot-tall saguaro cactus in the middle of the scorching hot Arizona desert."

103. N. P. M. P.

I am a two-time nuclear medicine patient and married priest.

104. NICKNAME

Who calls his lover-spouse Lou Lou La Belle *Cocoux Cocoux La Rue* Honolulu?

105. ANTIDOTE

Married priests are the antidote to excommunication.

106. PHONE

Whose wife's cell phone doesn't fit in her full "files"?

107. **AKA**

Whose wife is not his Alexandra Solzhenitsyna?

108. **CHARACTER**

Whose wife's soul is as soft and smooth as silk and satin, and her character stronger than the strongest steel?

CHAPTER FIVE

MISCELLANEOUS

109. **DECADENCE DEGREE**

Imperial Rome's pursuit of pleasure lasted longer than that of prerevolutionary France.

(See Will & Ariel Durant, *The Age of Voltaire*, pp. 292–29)

110. **REPARATION**

Lots of reparation needs to be done for one's distant, distant relatives (*conquistadores*): former dictator Leonidas Trujillo of the Dominican Republic and certain kindred clergy in high places.

111. **GUARD**

To be a school crossing guard is to be constantly vigilant, protective of all pedestrians, cyclists, and handicapped individuals. Listening to the radio, talking to friends on the street or on the phone, and neglecting one's post is *verboten* (prohibited), careless, and a waste of taxpayers' money.

112. **ADMIRATION**

Did you ever admire a Spanish Basque's French blue beret, and he gave it to you? Did you ever admire a Mexican married priest's silver medal and chain, and he gave them to you? What would have happened if you had paid a compliment to the owner of a magnificent Mercedes-Benz?

113. POLISH

Amazing what a little polish will do to one's beat-up blue-gray tennis shoes.

114. HERO

Many a married man has the hands of a hardworking artisan, the eyes of an artist, and the heart of a hero.

115. GUESS WHO?

He wears a red coat with white fur-trimmed sleeves, a red stocking cap with a white fur tassel, a black belt, and glossy black boots, has white hair, white eyebrows, a white moustache, a curly white and well-groomed beard, sparkling blue eyes, a jolly, oval face, and says, "Ho, ho, ho" with a Spanish accent, and comes from northern New Mexico every Christmas Eve. Who is he? He is Sanchez Claus, a close relative.

116. MORE THAN ABRAHAM

Monsignor John Corrigan, a Wyoming priest from Connecticut, used to say, "Father Pat Trujillo has more relatives than Abraham."

117. GREATNESS

One is greater than any criticism.

118. **WHY?**

Who is bemused and befuddled, but not bedraggled when a rich institution uses poor-quality paper to correspond with them?

119. **FILTHY FRIENDS**

Filthy friends have twice used the front steps for a table and chair, have discarded their banana peels, soiled napkins, and assorted garbage gunk in front of our house.

120. **BILINGUAL**

Have any of your cousins ever said, "You speak Spanish with an Irish accent"?

121. **RHYTHM**

Isn't it disconcerting, disturbing, and distressing to be interrupted when one has achieved a certain rhythm with the work at hand?

122. **ORIGINALITY**

A sign above a place where haircuts are given reads, "The Barber Shop."

123. **OPTION OR . . .**

In the presence of a priest's wife, a dentist friend said, "Don't forget to fulfill your husbandly duties." The priest responded, "Is that an option or an order?"

124. **UNAWARE**

How unaware we are of the hundreds of trillions of synapses in our 200-billion-cell brain.
(See Bruce Goldman, "Stunning Details of Brain Connections Revealed.")

125. **EJACULATION**

Back when, an ejaculation meant a short exclamatory prayer. Now, it means sexual ecstasy.

126. **MYSTERIOUS**

Some modern art begins with mystery because the artist does not always know what the object will be until after it is finished.

127. **TIT FOR TRANSPORTATION TAT**

A married priest and his wife met a kind, elderly white-haired gentleman while on the train in Holland in July of 2000. The priest told him, "I have owned seven cars since I was ordained in 1996." The senior citizen answered, "I've never owned an automobile, but I have owned four bicycles."

128. **UNEXPECTED**

Just when one gets into the rhythm of relaxation, one is called to some other activity.

129. **BEWARE**

If you must beware of me, must I also be wary of thee, too?

130. **SCARCITY**

One's English, like one's resources, is "too few."

131. **"KOONQUES"**

Every morning, one reads her "koonques," coffee grounds, but she doesn't always understand their meaning.

132. SUCCOR

May Ernest Hemingway help make our minds as nimble as our fingers.

133. KEEN COMPANIONS

Joseph Haydn and Samuel Clemens (Mark Twain) keep us company while we copy, edit, and revise.

134. WARDROBE EXQUISITE

One's tattered, torn, and threadbare bathrobe will last another twenty years if the spouse, who has threatened more than once to throw it in the garbage can, leaves it alone.

135. INDULGENCE

Some drink too much while others consume excessive sugar.

136. PUBLISHING

If others do most of the work, they get most of the money. If one does most of the work, then one reaps the rewards.

137. **COMICAL?**

What is more comical than one attempting to play Niccolò Paganini's "Variazoni sul Carnevale di Venezia" with the left hand when one is right-handed?

138. **THREE GRACES**

We want to grow older gracefully, cheerfully, and thankfully.

139. **UNCOMMON**

Most people put on their glasses, but others take theirs off to read.

140. **SAME**

With the rich, one wears poor clothes, and with the poor, one wears poor clothes.

141. **TOO MUCH?**

Some know as much history as can fit in a teaspoon.

142. **BROTHER BEES**

Our brother bees a few blocks from home make the best honey for the money.

143. **CHOLESTEROL-FREE**
Buffalo/bison is our best buy.

144. **MY MEDICINE**
For a burn in the bones, aloe vera in concentrated capsules from Mount Dora, Florida, soothes and tones.

145. **PART-TIMER**
A handicapable wife says, "If I can't get a part-time job cleaning outside windows in the Empire State Building, then I'll take a part-time job driving an eighteen-wheeler on icy mountain roads at night in Canada and Alaska in the wintertime.

146. **THE WORST**
Not to face oneself is the worst that could happen to anyone.

CHAPTER SIX

MORALITY

147. **ANTIRELIGIONISTS**

Atrocities, scandals, and foolishness cause many to shun religion and deny G-d.

148. **BADGE OF HONOR**

A mini-martyrdom is excommunication and name-calling by certain church officials and their controlling colleagues.

149. **COMES AROUND**

Time does not erase but only delays the memory of one's deeds.

150. **MARTYR**

If those responsible for the assassination of Pope John Paul I, Albino Luciani, in September 1978 could get away with it, then the cover-up of sacerdotal pedophilia must seem like a mere trifle.

151. **JUSTICE**

Apology is apropos for minor mistakes. Restitution is required for crimes committed.

152. **WHICH ONE?**
Of all the institutions, which one seems seriously
sexually deviant and neurotic?

153. **INFALLIBILITY/IMPOSSIBILITY**
To reform an institution whose head is infallible
seems impossible.

154. **PAR FOR THE COURSE**
Pedophile priests and celibate priest violators of
women are called "spiritual sons" by some of the
Roman Catholic hierarchy, while married priests were
defamed as "criminals."

155. **MASQUERADE**
The "Year of the Priest" is but insidious misinformation, putting the face of good priests over the
pernicious semblance of their former leaders and
colleagues.

156. **MARTYRDOM**
. . . is not just the killing of the body, but the wound-
ing of one's spirit and the defamation of character.

157. **JUSTNESS**

Is it better to let the Romans rot in their magnificent buildings, their splendid attire, and their suffocating secrecy or to attempt to reform them?

158. **HAUGHTINESS**

. . . is like an extremely fast, seemingly invincible, and dangerous sports car with a hair-trigger accelerator.

159. **SHAME**

To abandon, disown, and renounce one's own child for the sake of an institution is despicable.

160. **TOUCHÉ TOUCHÉ**

Protests increase while institutions continue in their injustice and scandal.

161. **LESSER OF TWO EVILS**

Mao Tse-tung, who apparently never brushed his teeth and whose gums were probably swollen with pus, had a cleaner mouth than the one who blames the sexual abuse of children and women on the devil. (See "Mao Tse Tung: Worst Hygiene in a Dictator")

162. **FOLLOW THE LEADER**

When celibate priests abandon their own children, they are only following the example of Siricius, who abandoned his wife and children in order to become pope in AD 385.

163. **ARROGANCE**

Who dares to don his white, demand absolute obedience, tout himself, and feign ignorance of sexual crimes committed by his subordinates?

164. **MASK**

Gentle-looking public faces, guardians of the flock, hide wild packs of dogs that rip out the throats of married priests' pensions.

165. **RIGHTNESS**

The roar of the lion of G-d is for justice for His People.

166. **TEMPORARY TRIUMPH**

When a good person is martyred, then filthy politics has triumphed . . . for now.

167. **HATRED'S HEAT**

A calm, long-lasting, smoldering, intense hatred is much more dangerous than spontaneous anger.

168. **HOPE**

When politicians regard the common good more than their personal advantage, then there is hope for the world.

169. **FRAUD**

How can an entity call itself a nonprofit organization when it collects massive amounts of money, a large portion of which is sent overseas for investment?

170. **MALICE**

Evil remains evil even if done by someone in high office.

171. **INTRINSIC EVIL**

The kidnapping by Pope Pius IX of a Jewish child, Edgardo Mortara, who was secretly baptized as a seriously ill infant without the consent of his parents, remains intrinsically evil.

172. **CORRUPTION**

Receiving a huge amount of money for charitable purposes from known narcotics dealers is despicable. Rewarding such a recipient with a high office and benefice shows corruption at the highest level and is an outrageous insult to humanity.

173. **TOTALITARIAN MENTALITY**

Do those who have not signed the Universal Declaration of Human Rights have hardened hearts and totalitarian mentalities?

174. **STATUS**

Why should any religion have to torture, maim, and kill to maintain its status?

175. **HISTORIC IRRESPONSIBILITY**

O the wonder of the spiritual life of "Saint" Augustine and others like him, who can have a child out of wedlock, disregard their own flesh and blood, and then shove their own progeny into oblivion.

176. **AMBASSADORS OF PEACE**

The great sultan Malik al-Kamil allowed Francis of Assisi into his presence, conversed with him, and even became his friend and brother. However, the warring popes of the time did not reciprocate by allowing any Muslim holy men into their presence. (See Paul Moses, *The Saint and the Sultan*, p. 14)

177. **REASONABLE?**

If the federal government is financially punishing committed senior citizen couples who get married by substantially reducing their Social Security benefits, then injustice is being hailed as a good.

178. **DISINFORMATION UNLIMITED**

Some believe that by making cutthroats saints their corruption is thereby forgotten.

179. **LOPSIDED JUSTICE**

Millions upon millions of dollars are being spent by US dioceses and religious orders to victims of clerical sexual abuse. However, about 66 percent of the above entities apparently do not see the injustice of denying married priests their pensions even to this day . . .

180. **BLASPHEMY**

To propagate lies for centuries and then claim that such is the work of the Holy Spirit is . . . blasphemy?

181. **PRIORITY**

Some are more interested in protecting property than in standing up for and protecting human rights.

182. **TRIPLETS**

Misinformation, lies, and deception belong to the same Machiavellian family.

183. **INCAPACITY TO ERR**

. . . implies the continuation of lies.

184. **SEXUAL MORES**

Abusive short-term relationships are preferred by too many rather than committed and loving long-term ones.

185. **EVIL TO THE CORE?**

Will there be a ban against the use of all rubber gloves because they are condoms for the hands, unnatural, and thereby intrinsically evil?

186. **SARDONICISM**

Religious felons have their gall when they dare label/ libel as criminals those who have committed no crimes.

187. **SCANDAL**

Who doesn't intensely dislike those who hide their crimes behind religion, thereby causing others to lose their faith?

188. **EXAMPLE**

Vile is he who teaches others ethics while his own character is contemptible.

189. **SCANDAL BIG-TIME**

Is the international magnitude of the sexual abuse scandal but another "proof" of the infallibility of the pope in matters of faith and morals?

190. **CONFUSED?**

By making the wrong people saints, is evil being sanctified?

191. **NEGLIGENCE**
Does our government neglect Native Americans, with whom it has broken almost all treaties made with them?

192. **JUSTICE THWARTED**
A teenager gets his girlfriend pregnant, and everyone knows about it. A clergyman gets his girlfriend pregnant, and lawyers secure a gag order on the woman . . .

193. **HINDSIGHT**
Do we understand now why a certain ecclesiastical dignitary refused to attend the funeral of six priests murdered by the Mafia in Sicily?

194. **PEDOPHILE PATRON SAINT**
Who is the Patron Saint of Pedophiles?

195. **HENCHMEN PATRON SAINT**
Who is the Patron Saint of Henchmen?

196. **HARDBALL**

It's easy for the bullyboys of the barrio to play hardball, to countersue when they have lots of money, influence, and power, and their opponent is financially weak.

197. **"SAINT" AMBROSE**

Is Ambrose, former Roman military general, the Patron Saint of Persecutors and Dictators?

198. **VIGILANCE**

Citizens, legislators, beware of those who influence penal and other laws for their own benefit.

199. **WHO CARES?**

Do anonymous powers care about Camden, New Jersey; Pine Ridge, South Dakota; Immokalee, Collier County, Florida; and the coal-mining towns of West Virginia? If so, how?

200. **SOCIAL JUSTICE**

Those who care about social justice belong to the Church, to All-h, to G-d, to *Meaning*, or are numbered among the just. Those who don't care belong to institutions.

201. **DEBAUCHERY**

Some believe that by calling others libertines they thereby deflect their own debauchery.

202. **"PRACTICED" POVERTY**

"The Vatican Bank has slightly more than 33,000 accounts, mostly in Europe, also including dioceses and religious orders around the world, and controls an estimated $7 billion in assets."

(John L. Allen, Jr., "A Vatican Watershed in Transparency," *National Catholic Reporter*, August 3–16, 201)

203. **AVARICE**

Some "hold in their hands almost all the wealth of the State. They are a miserly crew, always getting and never giving, they are continually hoarding their income to acquire capital."

(Will & Ariel Durant, *The Age of Voltaire*, p. 34)

204. **INTOLERANT SPIRIT**

"It is not the multiplicity of religions which has produced wars; it is the intolerant Spirit animating that one which believed itself in the ascendant."

(*"Considerations sur les causes de la grandeur de Romains et de leur decadence."*)

(See Will & Ariel Durant, *The Age of Voltaire*, p. 34)

205. **ATROCITIES' APEX**
2,700 Muslim prisoners within sight of their own
Muslim brothers were beheaded by King Richard the
Lionheart during the Third Crusade.
(See Paul Moses, *The Saint & the Sultan*, p. 67)

206. **POLITICAL EQUALITY?**
How can there possibly be political equality when
the wealthy can hire a plethora of lobbyists to unduly
influence our legislators?

207. **"SAINT" CONFUCIUS**
Voltaire "was ready to canonize Confucius who 'had
taught the Chinese people the principles of virtue five
hundred years before the founding of Christianity."
(See Will & Ariel Durant, *The Age of Voltaire*, p. 506)

208. **MORAL ROOTS**
A thousand years is no guarantee of the moral sound-
ness of an institution's roots.

209. **REVELATION**
Thanks to mass media, rot, putrefaction, and moral
decay are cutting through gold, glitter, and glamour.

210. **INTEGRITY**

Those in high places must answer the charges brought against them by SNAP (Survivors Network of Those Abused by Priests) and Amnesty International.

211. **WITNESS**

To bear witness is to show G-d's Face to the world.

212. **"SAINT" IRENAEUS**

Is "Saint" Irenaeus a forerunner of the enforcer of the Index of Forbidden Books and a model for The Inquisition?

(See http://southerncrossreview.org/2/gnostic.html. "Bishop Irenaeus of Lyon c. 180, wrote five volumes entitled *The Destruction and Overthrow of Falsely So-called Knowledge*. By the time of the Emperor Constantine's conversion in the fourth century, possession of books denounced as heretical became a criminal offense.")

213. **IMPRISONMENT**

How many women and men are imprisoned because their abandonment by their parents has turned their sadness into rage against society?

214. **BLINDNESS**

Vindictiveness can blind us in many areas.

215. **WOUNDS**

Institutions have been ravaged by leaders' insatiable vindictiveness, pomposity, bureaucracy, greed, and gossip.

216. **REINCARNATED INQUISITION**

Brutal inquisitional methods have been adopted by many regimes, democratic governments, and even by religious institutions.

217. **SLOPPINESS**

Doing the least is not an art, but mere laxity.

218. **H3**

To harbor, hide, and help pedophiles only serves to alienate more people from their faith.

219. **MARTYRS**

For telling the truth, some are strangled before being burned again at the stake like Italian Dominican friar Girolamo Savonarola. Others are burned by ridicule, derision, lies, and betrayal.

(See http://www.historytoday.com/richard-cavendish/execution-florentine-friar-savonarola)

220. **VENEER**

To perpetuate lies is hardly divine inspiration but rather diabolical daring.

221. **TUT TUT**

Some folks are very valid and highly licit, but dreadfully immoral.

222. **NICOLETO MACHIAVELLI**

Is Machiavelli the patron saint of power-hungry civil and religious leaders?

223. **VILIFICATION**

Those who vilify others think they can hide their own stigma of vilification.

224. **BAD SEED**

Avarice, avidity, covetousness, and greed are despicable quadruplets of the same egotistical lineage.

225. **ABUSE**

Power, position, and prestige often depose collegiality, cooperation, and the common good of the community.

226. **AVARICIOUSNESS**

Some financial institutions spend their government-gotten money on advertising, junk mail, and risky investments, but not on helping homeowners avoid foreclosure.

227. **SAME STATUS**

A slave owner, regardless of his philanthropy, is still a slave owner.

228. **ABANDONMENT**

Desertion of women who become pregnant by their celibate priest lovers is similar to the abandonment by institutions of those who dare disagree with discipline disguised as doctrine.

229. **PRECEDENCE**

Obedience still remains the greatest of virtues—out-stripping even charity and justice—when it comes to certain authority figures dealing with sex abuse scandals by pedophile clergy. Tragic.

230. **VERBAL ABUSE**

Denigration, degradation, derogation, belittlement, and mockery are forms of verbal abuse.

231. **LEGAL ABUSE**

To use the law for one's own self-serving purposes is abominable.

232. **ASSASSINATION**

Some good people are murdered; others suffer character assassination.

233. **JUSTICE ASKEW**

The rich have more than their fair share of the bread of justice while the poor are lucky to get the crumbs.

234. **WHOSE COUNTRY?**
Let us never allow the United States to become a
country of corporations, by corporations, and for
corporations.

235. **DISCERNMENT**
Obedience that does not take into account discernment of G-d's Will first and foremost, is shallow,
possessive, and domineering.

236. **EXONERATION**
Vindication of one's name and honor mean more than
monetary recompense.

237. **EQUITY?**
First-rate justice exists for the rich, and fourth-rate
justice for the poor. Shame. "*Shoah.*" "*Que verguenza.*"

238. **PRIMACY**
When obedience has primacy of place, then charity
and justice take second and third place.

239. **EQUAL?**
Some don't commit murder, just assassination by
gossip and chatter.

240. **DICTATORS**

Those who do not abide by their own constitution and bylaws are dictators.

241. **TRUMP**

Treachery is the trump card of malice.

242. **EVIDENCE TAMPERING**

To meddle with historical facts is criminal evidence tampering.

243. **IMBALANCE**

If legislators were as enraged about Joe Citizen's civil rights being violated when the NSA (National Security Agency) spied on his e-mails and telephone calls as they were when the spying turned on them, what a wonderful world 'twould be.

244. **DIFFERENTIATION**

Some don't know the difference between slander (calumny, detraction) and open, honest, and frank discussion.

245. **LAWYERS' CHALLENGE**

When the rule of law is bypassed in favor of the rules lawyers play by, then reform of the legal system is imperative.

246. **SCANDAL'S SCAR**

When injustice involves the Supreme Court, no legal loophole maneuvering will remove the scar of scandal.

247. **INJUSTICE'S LEGACY**

Avoidance of hurt feelings between prosecutor and defense attorneys hinders the pursuit of justice and leaves truth hidden, forgotten for years.

248. **NEGLIGENCE NIGHTMARE**

Toxic waste, which eventually finds its way into water, the air, and the food chain, is a continual negligence nightmare. Who's responsible? No one, of course, not even . . .

249. **BETRAYAL**

When loyalty trumps truth, the innocent bear the scar of loyalty's lash.

250. **HIDING PLACE**

Church is a dignified term and place behind which scoundrels hide.

251. **PARAGON**

An institution riddled with scandal can ill afford to teach justice, morals, and ethics.

252. **EXPLOITATION**

Exploitative executives must not only be bashed, but blamed and banished.

253. **VALUED VOW?**

What value is there in a vow that costs the innocent their integrity and their good name?

254. **SCAPEGOATS**

Those who are not puppet popes can expect no less than assassination in one form or another.

255. **MORE**

If evil men can be thorough in their malice, how much more efficient must good people be in their pursuit of truth, justice, and charity?

256. **SUPER SHAME**

A church official in public slapped a priest for taking a political position. Other ministers can meddle in the politics of other countries, but let a humble priest assist his weary country, and he was humiliated. When martyred Salvadoran Bishop Oscar Romero told the Pope John Paul II about the atrocities committed by the government, Pope John Paul II responded, "Well, now don't exaggerate. It is important that you enter into a dialogue with the government."
(See David Yallop, *The Power and The Glory: Inside the Dark Heart of John Paul II's Vatican*, Carroll & Graf, p. 77)

257. **DENIAL**

When some people can't resolve issues, they resort to subversion.

258. **FATALITY**

For those steeped in corruption, there is no choice but to continue in their decadence and do some good as a distraction to others.

259. **LAST ONES**

Money grabbers should be the last ones to critique and criticize capitalism.

260. **UGLY CRIME**

Whether one year or 1,300 years pass, a crime is still a crime.

261. **FINGER-POINTING**

How much easier it is for religious to blame capitalism than to point fingers at themselves.
(See Kevin Clarke, "Pope Francis is Not a Marxist, but Make No Mistake: He Will Challenge the World's Leading Capitalist Power.")

262. **OUTLOOK**

If the poor of the United States seem like the middle class to the extremely poor of the world, then the way some clergy live must seem like the billionaires' club.

263. **MORE CAPITALISTIC?**

What institution is more capitalistic than . . . ?

264. **UNBALANCED SCALE**

To suspend an elderly missionary priest indefinitely for sending the Sunday collection to the poor of South America without the bishop's permission is to err seriously on the side of severity rather than on the side of mercy, compassion, and understanding.

265. **EVENHANDEDNESS?**
To crush an eight-year-old's right hand with the weight of an automobile for stealing food does not fit the crime with the punishment.

266. **ETHICS MEASUREMENT**
When the bottom line for anyone is money rather than the common good, then his or her ethics fit nicely into a thimble.

267. **VILE**
When obedience takes precedence over justice and charity, a sad state of affairs ensues.

CHAPTER SEVEN

POETRY

268. **DRUG DEALERS**
Bloody
machetes, bloated egos, brave
loaded guns intimidate the poor,
the defenseless
children.

269. **OPTIMISM**
Delicate light-green cycads and Korean Rock Ferns
Reddish-green needle ferns
Broad green-leaved pathos plant
tinged beige-white centers
Broad dark-green, light-green arrowed
red-veined leaves
Forty delicate miniature purple floral bassinets
Eight light-green, orange miniature shamrocks
Mingled in firmly woven dark-brown wicker basket
Hold expectations together.

270. **EXPECTATION**
Dream's
high-sky brilliant acrylic rainbow,
majestically splendored in dreary, dark, damp days
that hide hallowed mystery, harkens hidden
happiness.

271. **ENVISION**
Prophet's pivotal power
People pray, progress, dare not die
Silently clamor for life, for life
Trumpet
in near despair: "I am G-d's creation.
I will not be discarded.
Hope is hello's power."

272. **ROME**
Disinformation
bought by widows' mite
mocks married priests
yields scandal's scalpel
slits financial throats.
Disinformation
ensures, extols religious obedience
from reverend vassal rascals.
Rome mocks married priests.

273. **FOOLISH?**
Adidas sandals in snow
Bagged blue tennis shoes in tow
New van topped with two-inch snow
Lazy, foolish ones?
No, no
no.

274. **MIGHTY MEMENTO**

Multitudinous memories
tears, heartaches,
confusing conflicts
deep dismay
dark discouragement,
almost deadly despair
white sorrow avalanches
bury a lone mountain tree
unbroken presence
shows forth faith
in the One
who blessses,
sustains, and brings us to
this moment.

275. **ENIGMA**

My time, talent, and money
they take.
My sacerdotal state
they forsake.
On me, scorn, derision, defamation
lie.
Hopeless, seemingly useless my
cry.

276. **SNOW**
Heavy
heavy white, hoary snow
Bends, bends, tears, rips, topples trees
Refreshes, replenishes, refurbishes, renews
Invigorates, decorates, redecorates, positions
fine, finishing touches on earth's dress for
spring

277. **QUEST**
My own mortality I face
With gratitude, with hope, with grace.
Each breath, each life breath my last—here
Divine Breath, breathes in me—near
Expectation, diminished fear
My vision, purpose ever clear

278. **INNER ME**
In
inner conscience
memory webs unravel
composite slick strand stories
inner conscience
shakes, sinks, marks, mars
me.

279. **ONENESS**

In love,
by love bound
with, for, by me in accord
to lose my Sovereign, I cannot afford
better my heart should pierce, impale, a sword
my body benign beauty bound
skin to bone, ear embraces sound
tongue, teeth, palate, mouth—quadruplets one
Nth Power Synapses, galaxies
millions, billions, trillions
multiplied.

280. **R.I.P**

Sadness
Sinks, slowly slides down my soul
Mourning mounds
Mount grief upon grief
Avalanche overruns me
A lone tree overwhelmed, buried
By heavy white sorrow
Compelling memories press in upon me
My beloved's voice heard
Almost aloud, unreachable
In my heart, my love walks slowly
Leaves an indelibly etched portrait
Slithering slabs of regret shake, crush me
Into the Powerful, All-Enveloping
All-Gentle, All-Gracious
G-d.

281. **PRAYER'S PROTECTION**

Pray in the morning
Adore, praise G-d, sing
Solid rock invisible shield
Archangels all around me wield
Michael, to my right, protect me
Gabriel through me Divine messages shared
Uriel before me, prepare me, prepared
Healer Rafael behind others, me, healed.

282. **RICHARD SMOLEV**
Indomitable Spirit
Breathes my mind
My fingers, vocal cords, lungs, legs, arms, and hands
Refuse to succor, to help, to move me
Racked body smashes my will, grinds my nerves
Almost . . . suffocates my Indomitable Spirit

283. **OPENNESS**
Meet face-to-face.
Fear not disgrace.
If one in discourse proven wrong
Apology—written, spoken, or in song.

284. **AIN'T BLACK**
You ain't black, Honey.
You ain't black. You dark, dark brown
Your boots pitch black. Your long skirt jet black
Your braided hair deep ebony black
But your skin, Honey, like my Mama's,
Is deep, deep dark, dark cinnamon.

285. **M. JANE**
Mary Jane, mysterious Mary
My complex, consigned companion
Foe, friend, seductive, illusive, secretive
Secretive siren friend, healer, hellion

286. **SECRETIVE SINS**
Dastardly deeds live in shame
Clandestine crimes bear no name.
Simple, normal life seems
Hidden within, conscience steams.
Hallowed face hides history's fare
Your brother's eyes betrayal bear.

287. **TASHI, TIBET**
Traumatized four-year-olds
faces swollen, bear refugee burdens beyond their
weight.
Numbing-cold tender fingers grasp the Dalai Lama.
Sounds of prayer wheels only rarely heard.
My memory's eye beholds Tibet's rape,
three thousand ravaged monasteries.
Jagged Himalayan home cannot hide hideous
Communist crimes.
My memory's eye beholds
raped refugees in a foreign land.
Tibetans, meditative, still, remain
tranquil waters
probe turmoil depths in total surrender to peace.

288. **CONTEMPLATION**
Music in my deafness,
symphony in silence,
masterpiece in my void.
Illusive transparent notes
strike harp fibers of my mind.

289. **POETRY'S PRIZE**
Poetry speaks its own language—
words, laser lights
curative, disfigurative
heal, seal, burn
write words still hot,
live what you write and not what you're not,
strive for the olympic poetic laurel.

290. **VOCATION**
My vocation
Rolls, roams, rambles me
down the hard-copy highway,
burst forth lightning-fueled
idea vistas on ethereal roads
siphoned into sonorous sonnets
silently invite screen wilderness,
cruise converging crossways,
encapsulates volumes,
minimum words capture maximum moments
proudly present truth's pageantry,
picture the soul body's pain,
unveil innocence's beatific face,
journey arduous, perilous way
in one sonnet step,
encase evil's enormity in iambic pentameter,
disconcert doubts
despoil despotic plausible position,
plumb pleasure's pomegranate's *"pièce de résistance"*
and pain's pilloried porcupined performance,
live despair's daring drive
in death's defying disturbance,
traverse tranquility's turmoil
in the strength of silence.

291. **VOCATION'S APEX**
Wildest soul stirrings of my being
mingle with dry tears' resolve,
bears humiliation's defeat
rises in unconquered determination,
lunges forward for truth's sake.
Slakes achievement's thirst
propels my inner plane
to excellence's dizzying heights:
sweaty nervous palms, clenched tightened teeth,
pursed purpled lips, finely furrowed forehead,
Steel one's ego against adulation's honor,
perceives, prunes, reinforces truth's tree
in vanity's rubbish while seeking other's gain
in adversity's unspeakable malice—sidesteps the
cockroaches and rats of pretense.
Clasps, grasps faith's fine fiber
in work's worrisome web woven wondrously well
in circadian rhythm's dedication engraved in one's
universal soul,
knows no limits to goodness's multifaceted
    expressions
manifest in life's seeming trivialities.
Shows soul signs of beginning anew,
new starts, old defeats, manifold entries to enfold,
beholds simplicity's artistry,
unravels creation's web
through inopportune moments.

292. **PASSOVER**

From sacred to passé
Super Satan supersedes purposeful angel
young marriageable woman discarded for virgin
excommunication excises inclusivity
celibacy tramples family fidelity
conformist persecution burns truth's challenge
Light without dethrones Light within
Scurrilous slander bumps Eighth Commandment
Sabbath disowned by Lord's Day
Kidnapping's crowned Prince canonized

293. **MODELS**

One cloth away from nudity
Models strut their exhibitionist (voyeuristic) stuff
Beach attire indistinguishable from informal wear
Models walking disjointedly
Brazen look, false stare
clothes unmake the woman.

294. **STRAW MAN**

I am a straw man,
tightly-woven straw man
bound by this world's discards.
Compressed, intense straw
comprises me.
My billion-trillion dust ashed relatives
encircle me.
Stone, earth, pebbles, desert, boulders,
mighty mountains speak their silence
to my soul.
Calumnious arrows rip my finely fibered frame
still I remain treachery's timely target.
I am a straw man.
Humoring fire-resistant silicon's coating
shields off anger's fire.
I am a straw man.

295. **UNITY**
Ruah, Ru,
Spiritus, Espíritu,
Esprit,
Unity,
One
contra positions
deadly uniformity.
Life's breath bursts
complacency's illusion,
beckons, buttresses
sincerity's quest
for
truth.

296. **HELL'S CHELATION**
Multiple cruelties, tragic brutalities,
scream through the ages.
Cold, callous conniving instigators,
Perspicacious crime perpetrators
Oh, pompous, pernicious, philandering misfits
hide behind
cassocks, robes, cinctures,
Stolen Hebrew yarmulkes,
ivory Florsheim shoes.

297. **MARRIAGE REFLECTION**
Love's light,
G-d's Affection, Allah's Tenderness,
Has His Light of Love bestowed upon us
Openness to Allah
manifests kindness
understanding
dedication
to each other,
to all.
May our years together be many,
our months filled with gladness,
our days with joy,
our hours with hope,
our minutes with thankfulness,
our seconds with passion.

298. **GOOD (A TRIPLE TETRACTYS)**
Peace
Shalom
Do G-d's Will.
Now is precious.
Procrastination always talks the walk.
Intentionality needs your backbone.
Face your problems.
Shine brightly
with gain.
Peace.

299. BON (A TRIPLE TETRACTYS)

Bon
Salam
Oi jour d'hui
est precious (est le melior)
Saleh allekum. Allekum sad dam.
Et nous sommes bonnes parce que Dieu est tres bon.
Bon

300. PEACE

Peace.
Shalom.
Do G-d's Will.
Now is precious.
Procrastination always talks the walk.
Intentionality needs your backbone.
Face your problems.
Chelation
is yours.
Peace.

301. LAZY BIRD

With neither guts nor gumption
to clean up after his dog,
he yells, "Who in hell are you to check up on me?"
"I'm citizen ass. Who are you?" I replied.
He turned his dirty, unshaven face toward his dog and
walked away.

302. **MARCO POLO ME**

I am from Thatta, Pakistan
Kasgar, Uyghur
Danlataban, Afghanistan.
I am a Tibetan Champa,
a Mongol horse breeder,
a Dravidian from Kerala,
a young beauty from Sigiriya, Sri Lanka,
a seven-year-old from the Lisu tribe in Yunnan
a M'nong from Vietnam.
I've traveled from western Kazakhstan, Azerbaijan,
seen the Taurus and Pontus Mountains,
and lived near the yellow-brown minaret
in the camel tuape hills of Cappadocia.

303. **EXHORTATION**

Breathe in the past,
exhale the present,
Lungs fill in the future.
History lives in me.

304. **POETRY BIRTH**
Poetry
begins
inchoately
ends
resplendently
puts into
carefully
weighed
words
what the
Architect
Artist
does.
This
is
poetry.

305. **DO**
Two letters
mountains of meaning
Polite
Emphatic
Auxiliary
Active
Passive?

306. **SPANISH RELATIVES**
The Arabs
look at me with squinty, skeptical eyes.
The Jews
throw back their heads
open wide their eyes.
Both say,
"Who is this
who writes our words?"

307. **TRAGIC RONNY**
Reverend Father
always right
targets children, trafficks trust
turns "Ronny" innocent into two Ronnys.
Ronny told
Mommy and Daddy knew
approved Father's rape.
"Wasn't Reverend Father
always right?"
Ronny had been told.
Devout, scared anguished,
tortured Ronny
None to turn . . . to.
"Why do I have to hurt so much?
I hate Mom and Dad.
I hate G-d."
Conniving curates
excuse
enable
abuser priest
repeat rapist
of eleven-year-old Ronny
on too many other Ronnys.

308. ***HATUEY***

Ciboney cacique
Guanahacabibes guardian
Arawak agglutinate
sub-Taino
Taino tepa template
Conquistadors' gold greed resistor
Human burning torch
Sears flesh
Boils blood
Open-air baked bones
Arawak's ashes sanctify
Curse Cuba's sand
Soul unsullied by Spanish Gold
Eternity's fee
pale with Spanish
pillage, ridicule, rape, murder
"Tighten the cords, light the fire!
I will share no heaven with hell's heathens!"
Ashes to sky
Ashes, waters blue, nurtured plants
Enriched blessed soil, Hatuey
Ciboney, Guanahacabibes, Arawak, sub-Taino, Taino
Hatuey

309. **VINDICATION**
Of thyself
be still.
Time's tried test will prove
thee true.
Thine honor defend not.
Others bearing truth
defend thee best.

310. **MY FATHER**
Fine
silver stripes
from my Father's head
reflect the sun's rays
onto his worn-out sofa.
"Pretty soon *murió*,"
he says.
"I will *die* soon."
He closes his eyes
his peacefully stoic face
seems not to move.
His dark blue overalls
cover his black and white checkered flannel shirt.
Strong, rugged, well-versed man
struggles for yet another breath.
Too many Camels have trampled his lungs.

311. TIPPERARY WILD ROSE

Curly brown ochre-burnt-sienna hair, serene golden
hazel eyes
Kuba cloth green skirt, double set pearls
Men sigh when she walks by
My Tipperary wild rose
faint freckles, cinnamon-brown specks,
delicately dance on her sharp Gaelic nose
Red apple lips surround her ivory-white smile
her mature eyes
understand my timidity.
Gently her hands assure, strengthen, assuage
my hesitant heart.
My Tipperary wild rose of Ros Cré.

312. THE TWIN

I am Ernest Patali
other brother of James Yee
I, too, like he a chaplain be
Ruined career by General's lie
Aiding brother Muslims agonized cry
"Guantánamo chaplain traitor!" paranoia's cry
Better to sacrifice one than the rest to die.
Yee can go, Yee can go.

313. FREEDOM'S PRICE

One, himself
a self-inflicted gouged out eye
Another, an amputated finger
A third, stomach partially disemboweled
A fourth,
petroleum injected leg veins . . .
a lifetime invalid
Another his testicles
and penis cut off
Pain
their lightened load

314. BROTHER WIND

Whimsical
Wyoming wind wisks me away
Whining wind, whirls me up, over, beyond
the wild Wind River Range
Wild wolf's wooing invisible call
Spirals to heaven
Pounds my heart's ear
Shakes, shakes earth's soul
My wild whimsical Wyoming wind
Whining wind, whirls me up, over, beyond
the desert's dry dromedaries
at Camel's Back, southwestern Wyoming
My wild whimsical Wyoming wind.

315. **WILD PEACE**

Ask me, Sunset,
Mountain wild, things peace,
Wild peace.
There, Mountain.
March early there.
Cold prosody march,
Zigzag day snow.
Prosody Mountain,
Pavilion Spring,
Early Morning March.
Faith cold poetics
Hamlets between two.
Mademoiselle Morning Mountain
Eloise Wild, Pity G-d.
Blackberry Wild
Over the Woods
Through The River
Face My Amputated Abelard.
Cold Night, Sacred Temple
Pity Poison Death Tree
Melpomene Wears the Eyes of Eloise.

316. MACHIAVELLIAN CYCLE
Revenge the dead
inquisition the living.
Truth enslaved to power.
Holy hirelings,
Lateran lackeys, rape the rose
hideous henchmen
inphallibly incestuous
arrogance, obedience primal prizes
dastardly demons declared dogmatic darlings.

317. INSTITUTION'S FACE
The g(c)rime of the ages
is upon you, church
in the center of town,
dark, foreboding, arrogant
architecture.
Gawking people
wander in,
walk away, walk away.
Church
in the center of town
piercing pinnacle in the heart
of Rome
close to mammon, far from home.

318. **CATHAR MEMENTO**
From
Toulouse
to Foix
to Montsegur's
Cathar Castle
Hidden history's horrors
Inquisition's iniquity, caress
lies boldly bare
in my soul's
bed.

319. **MARRIED PRIEST MARTYRDOM**

(To the tune of "Have You Ever Been Across the Sea to Ireland")

I. Well Pope Urban II forced upon us his ways,
    and blamed us for being what we are.
    By the sword, he wrenched us from home
    and family
    and made slaves those who honored
    their wives.

II. Our homes, land, possessions, and our
     children
     savagely, brutally ripped away.
     My wife became the prince's property
     and concubine became her given name.

III. Well white robes hid all debauchery,
      later confessed, forgiven, repeated.
      But Mass was offered for all G-d's people
      with freshly washed, anointed
      celibate hands.

IV. My beloved ones became serious signs
     of sin,
     forbidden fruits, father's frustration.
     Forbidden I was to hold, visit, talk to them.
     I saw them see me with their sad, sad eyes.

V. My devoted wife fed and clothed our
    children
    with money made from easy beds.
    In time, they stopped going to church to
    see me.

My precious wife, now a prostitute's price.

VI.   Our eldest son became a criminal.

At sixteen, he was hanged before our eyes.

The other went insane with his constant,
why, why?

But I continued my celibate debauched life.

VII.   My drinking and carousing were excusable.

VIII. Christ's courage and His valor were
not mine.

Now I wish that then I had proclaimed
so boldly
with every breath, every ounce of strength
I had:

IX.   "Let all of Rome's torches burn my
body black.

Let Rome crush my head like sanguine
grapes.

Let Rome defame, malign, and slander
my name

but it will never, never make my wife
a whore.

X.   My children will never be nameless bastards
hiding crimes behind Rome's religious
robes."

And G-d's people will respect, revere,
and proclaim:

"He was a saint, a martyr of a man."

320. **LETHARGY**
Fumbling zombie,
no pen, no paper.
Interest—none.
Warms a seat,
chills his soul,
spreads
lethargy's contagion.

321. **MADELEINE T.'S SON REMEMBERED**
Oh, remembered dead,
Your prevailing presence pervades,
pierces my soul
echoes my voice
suffers, suffers sad stories . . .
Suffering and death test my faith.

322. **RUGGED ROCKIES**

I am the rugged Rocky Mountains
Old, snow cold, soul-warmed
Petrified mighty mold.
Wrinkled, rambling rugged white capped
Furrowed, rugged
Rocky Mountains.
Perpetual peaks
Birth the Uintas, La Sierra,
San Juan Mountains, La Plata, La Sangre de Cristo.
Terrible tundra.
Triple mile-high cloud sky companion
Majestically mighty meditative twin Swiss Alps sister.
I am the rugged Rocky Mountains.

323. **SUFICIENCE**

Silence
Patience
Sapience
Valience
Suficience
Quel plus?

324. **LOVE IN MARRIAGE**
A
finely tuned friendship.
Husband and wife
twin musicians
of
the same instrument.
Each
carefully adjusting
the
violin strings
of
communication.
Practice
makes
a
perfect polyphony.

325. **CONCILIATION**
Mediation
weaves wondrous webs
of peace.
Stitches, stretches strands
of hope
captures cynicism signs
of
contorted care.
Inverts insult
to
empathy
restructures ravenous rage
into
real recognition
understands unnerving
entities
perceives powerful principles
behind
bullish behavior.

326. **MYSTERY**

Don't have much time
but
have ALL TIME.
Don't have much space
but
ALL SPACE is mine.
PRECIOUS PRESENCE
PERMEATES
me
PERMANENTLY.

327. **VISUAL FEAST**

Throughout
France, Belgium, in Holland,
multiple fields green, yellow-beige growing grain.
Light, dark greenery,
mile after mile, after mile
Nature encounters, invigorates, makes me smile.

328. **MANHATTAN MOUNDS AND MOUNTAINS**

Gray

Transparent glass

Brown pyramidal

Carnegie Tower

Green-white shaped city domed spire

White-green black Cape Canaveral launching site

Reflect multilevel motion-picture marquees

Transparent

Light

Green

Squared trapezoidal topped structure

Dons twin white triangles

Atop white/green East/West rectangles

Long rectangular dark-green square glass plates

Intersperse

White/grey horizontal squares

Multibeige

Skyscrapers

White long rectangular

Multiple layered

Tridimensional towers

Giant light-ochre/beige

White green-gray pencil World Wide Plaza

Beige/black/brown assorted

Shaped Magnificence

West

Inn

Glazed dark-brown

Deep-turquoise horizontal striped

White diagonal lines
Gray square glass sheets
Purple/turquoise, navy-blue striped
Two-tone-green turquoise
Tiered
Light-blue
Structure
Black/white
Slender-striped
Paineta Española
Chrysler Building
Verizon
Red-checkered edifice
My
Kaleidoscopic
Mountain range
of brick, glass, and mortar.
Dark-blue
Green-blue
Scarlet-pink, red, yellow-green,
Deep-purple lit top
Intersperses
One
Perpetual
Cubic rainbow
W
Redpecker
Hotel
Aloft ivory
Ghost-gray

Slender rectangles
Cold-gray spired
Robust sentinel
Square-shouldered robot
Two-toned, sand-brown edifice
Prince crowned
Sand-yellow guardian
Aztec purple-brown Pyramid
Turquoise-green rectangles
Dress four-sided
Three beige yellow-striped
Light-gray, white steppe
Tiered complex
Maroon
Brown-ochre pinnacle
Olive burlywood mesa minor
Burnt sienna
Gold-ochre precipice
Circular encased
Beige rectangular tube
Orange-red brown
White top banded building
Gray-turquoise
White syringe
White-gray
Crest-banded scarlet, brown
Elongated rectangle
Inner
Sanctus
Sanctorum

Raw-umber complex.

329. **MANHATTAN MOUNTAIN RANGE**
Green-turquoise
Trapezoidal triangular
Apexed masterpiece
Light-beaver-brown
Beige-Peru, Chinese
Twin pagoda
Pinnacled castle
Tiered, towered, bejeweled
Hudson River steel, brick,
Glass, mortar Mountain Range
My spired
Multitiered brick, glass
Steel, Mortar Mountains
Castle mountained edifices
Silhouette
Silent skies
Pierce
Calm virgin
Clouds.

330. **OBITUARY TESTAMENT**
When I'm laid in my plain pine casket, place my tallit
near my right shoulder, my gold-threaded black kafiya
& aqel near my left shoulder, my rosary beads in my
left hand, my Buddhist prayer beads in my right hand,
around my right wrist, my leather Makah Indian
bracelet, and on the inside casket lid, my proverb
"Multinational" (589).

331. **HIGH ROAD**
I must get out of a rut
Or forever be a nut, nut
Ascend, ascend take the road high
Hurdles fear not; confront the sky.

332. **TROG**
Trog the frog from the Land of Blog.
Daily frisk fingers jump, jump, and jog
Touch, press encrypted plateaus
Letters to words, sentences blog book blogs
Blog, blog a website right.
Press on, press on many unknown hills
Delight, discover, refresh, sharpen skills

333. **DISAPPOINTMENT**
Who taught
celibate priests ethics:
cover-up evil
silence victims
expel
protesters?

CHAPTER EIGHT

POLITICS

334. **GOVERNMENT**
"Government is necessary, but it fails in its function if it is not based on virtue in ruler and ruled."
(Will & Ariel Durant, *The Age of Voltaire*, p. 34)

335. **IF**
. . . both Democrats and Republicans were as concerned about reducing their salaries, their insurance and pension benefits, and the national debt as they are about bickering with one another, what a wonderful nation 'twould be.

336. **GARBAGE AND POLITICS**
Garbage, politics at its worst, flattery, and lies differ very little from one another.

337. **HODGEPODGE POLITICS/EDUCATION**
When politics at its worst dictate educational policy, then poor student performance is the consequence.

338. **GARBAGE**
Politics at its worst is garbage.

339. **LOADED GUN OR POISON?**

When politicians play politics with education, learners lose.

340. **VERILY VERMIN**

Garbage dumps and politics at its worst are the breeding ground of rats.

341. **GOVERNMENT RESPONSIBILITY**

"The function of government is not to dominate the individual, but to widen the opportunities for his development."

(Will & Ariel Durant, *The Age of Voltaire*, p. 40)

CHAPTER NINE

PRAYER

342. **SUFI SELF**
One needs to be turned upside down until all the
foolishness falls out.

343. **CONCORD**
Some cannot articulate, but their lives demonstrate
that they are in harmony with and have the universe
as their home and nearest relative.

344. **EITHER OR**
If one does not spend sufficient time with G-d each
day, then one's other activities will spin a web of
entrapment.

345. **THE ORDINARY**
. . . is Extraordinary.

346. **MYSTERY**
G-d is the Infinitesimal, Infinite Galaxy of Galaxies
Who is above, below, around, and within every atom,
molecule, and cell of one's being.

347. **SOLUTION**
One who deals with problems all day long, but does not immerse him- or herself in and enjoy Silence, soon becomes part of the problem.

348. **THE LEAST AND THE MOST**
To pray for others is the Least and the Most we can do.

349. **DOUBLE ROLE**
The Archangels are not only bodyguards but soul guardians.

350. **REWARD**
The closer to G-d, the keener and stronger we are.

351. **LISTEN**
Pay attention to the prophetess's premonition.

352. **UNDER ONE'S NOSE**
Saints speak surprisingly in Silence.

353. **THE SPIRITUAL LIFE**

. . . grows as silently as one's toes, skin, hair, and fingernails.

354. **ELOHIM/ALL-H**

Elohim/All-h encompasses, enmeshes, enraptures, engulfs, inebriates, and enthralls us. *Elohim, All-h, Tu, est trés grande.* (G-d, You are Grand.)

355. **G-D**

. . . IS TIME, the INCALCULABLE MEASURE OF MOTION/MOBILITY.

356. **ONE**

. . . is our physical, emotional, mental, and spiritual CENTER.

357. **SUFICIENCE (SUFFICIENCY)**

Patience, valience. Deux est ma SUFIENCE. (Patience, Valor. G-d is my SUFFICIENCY.)

358. **ALPHA AND OMEGA**

G-d is the First One we run to when we need help, and the Last One to be loved.

359. MASTERMINDED

. . . means being led by the Master.

360. SUPERB LINGUIST

The Master Linguist creates and masters over 5,000 languages and a multitude of dialects.

361. LESSON

One must live every lesson learned.

362. APEX

The Apex is G-d.

363. REFLECTIVE WALKING

To walk reflectively is to reduce one's blood pressure and to fulfill the third injunction of the Prophet Micah, "Walk humbly with your G-d."

364. THANKFULNESS

We are grateful for the lessons of the past: for those which have raised us to the very heights of inspiration, and for those which have almost destroyed our souls.

365. **LOGIC?**

If nothing is impossible, then G-d must be
SOMEONE/THING.

366. **SHARING**

. . . is nourishment.

367. **SAY AND PRAY**

They sound alike but two letters make them an
Eternity apart.

368. **NECESSITY**

The older one becomes, the more the need for silence
and contemplation.

369. **WEDLOCK**

G-d is closer than one's breath. G-d is one's Breath.

370. **SIX BLESSINGS**

One can see sounds, hear pictures, feel eternity, taste
thoughts, smell and sense the Spirit.

371. **ADORATION**

To praise G-d is one's purpose, responsibility, challenge, opportunity, blessing, and fulfillment.

372. **APPRECIATIVENESS**

To accept one's situation in life while doing one's best is a blessing superb.

373. **REFLECTION**

Creativity is indeed a powerful prayer.

374. **GOLD**

Prayer is the frankincense, myrrh, and gold we offer G-d.

375. **NOURISHMENT**

Truth, like food, takes time to digest.

376. **DEVELOPMENT**

Truth, like a seed, takes time to be nourished, to grow, yield fruit, and be harvested.

377. **EXTREME**

G-d is the Greatest and the Least.

378. **I. S. P.**

G-d is Intelligence Supreme Plus.

379. **E. E. E.**

G-d is the Excellent Engineer of Engineers.

380. **A. A. A.**

G-d is the Absolute Architect of Architects.

381. **U. A. A. A.**

G-d is the Unique Artist of Artists and Artisans.

382. **DIVINE BREATH**

Life is the Divine Breath.

383. **D. D. D.**

G-d is the Divine Doctor of Doctors.

384. **P. P. E. P.**

G-d is the Psychiatrist *Par Excellence* of Psychiatrists.

385. **V. A. V.**

The Value of All Values is G-d.

386. **DISCERNMENT AND PRAYER**
Collegiality implies discernment and prayer.

387. **S. S. SCI.**
The Superb Scientist of all Scientists is G-d.

388. **M. M. M. M.**
My Most Meaningful Moment is G-d.

389. **M. C. C. C.**
The Master Charismatic Chemist of all Chemists is G-d.

390. **INTERACTIVE/INTRA-ACTIVE**
Interactive/Intra-active is G-d.

391. **CREDAL DISTINCTION**
Belief is more intellectual, while faith is profound acceptance.

392. **ENERGY**
G-d is Energy, and Prayer is the Connecting Cable.

393. **BOTH**

G-d is Both Inner and Outer Time and Space.

394. **CHANGE**

G-d is the Unchangeable Change.

395. **DEPENDENCE**

All power sources depend on the Omnipotent One.

396. **D-DAY PREP**

One is never too young to prepare for his or her death day.

397. **WEAVER**

Masterfully weaving together the galaxies of galaxies, all of chemistry's minerals and compounds, and all the DNA of all living organisms is the Master Weaver.

398. **GRIP**

Earnest prayer strengthens one's grip on the Timeless, Thorough Thread of Life.

399. **OPPORTUNITY**
An interruption may not be so much an interruption
as Inspiration's Opportunity.

400. **INCONSUMABLE**
The Inconsumable Fire is G-d.

401. **CAMOUFLAGE**
G-d, Prayer, the Spiritual Life, our deceased and living
relatives, animate and inanimate objects all participate in THE PERFECT CAMOULFLAGE.

402. **MERCIFUL MASTER**
G-d is our Merciful Master, our Perfect Peace.

403. **COMPLETE CYCLE**
We belong to G-d and to Him/Her we are returning.

404. **ID**
Who identifies more with my breathing, my seeing,
my hearing, my tasting, my touching, and my sense of
smell with their billions of cells than G-d?

405. **GRATITUDE**

May one's life be one continuous act of gratitude to G-d.

406. **ELECTRICIAN**

The Master Electrician of all electricians is G-d.

407. **TREASURE**

Prayer enables us to tap into the vast Treasure Trove of Poems which the Most Powerful Poet is.

408. **G. P.**

To bear witness to truth is to reflect G-d's Presence.

409. **ALL IN ONE**

Every particle of one's being contains one's Whole Being.

410. **TRANSCENDENCE**

To transcend sight and sound and our other three senses, is to enter into them more deeply.

411. **TIME TRAVEL**
Intelligent Life exists outside and inside of our universe(s).

412. **INFLUENCE**
Prayer is the Energy that influences untold millions in untold ways.

413. **VERB**
There exists only one most powerful verb: IS, and we all participate in IT.

414. **FAITH**
"He knows what He is about." I don't.
(From John Henry Cardinal Newman, "Some Definite Service." See http://www.appleseeds.org/Newman_My-Mission.htm)

415. **MULTIFORM PRESENCE**
The Lord takes on the Form of Air, Light, one's eyes, and more.

416. **CREATOR MARVELOUS**
If the Lord can create billions and billions of creatures, then He/She can take on a trillion-plus forms.

417. **ABSORPTION**

The Lord, like luxurious lotion, is absorbed into one's skin.

418. **PREPARED**

To the Lord, we come with empty pockets and a full heart.

419. **MASTER PLUMBER**

The Master of Master Plumbers is G-d.

420. **MANY SPLENDORED**

The Lord is our Many-Splendored One.

421. **VENTRILOQUIST**

One is the dummy; the Lord is the Ventriloquist.

422. **OPTION**

Only a Strength stronger than death can handle death.

423. IMPOSSIBLE?

When one finds oneself in a seemingly impossible situation, think of Abraham, who told his son Isaac, "The Lord will provide." (*Genesis* 22:8)

424. PEN

She is the pen with which the Wondrous Writer writes prophecy.

425. FLUTE

I am the flute through which the Divine Breath plays Magnificent Music.

426. COMPANY

May Prayer, Peace, Perseverance, and Patience permeate everything we do.

427. SIGHT

May the Lord always be our Eye/I.

428. INSTRUMENT

We are the willing instrument through which the Lord makes marvelous music, lovely lyrics, and potent proverbs and poetry.

429. **LIBERTY**

Letting go and letting G-d leaves us in Liberty.

430. **STRONGER**

Prayer, simple and sincere, begins a chain reaction stronger than nuclear fusion.

431. **ART**

. . . is a finely creative expression of prayer.

432. **THE UNIVERSAL**

The Grandest Galaxy over all galaxies, the Universal of universes, is G-d.

433. **SUPREME SYNAPSE**

The Supreme Synapse over the more than 700 trillion synapses of the human brain is G-d.
(See "700 New Synapses Every Single Second")

434. **COMPLETE CELL**

The Most Complete Neuron over the billions and billions of neurons in the human brain is G-d.
(See http://www.forbes.com/sites/arlenewein-traub/2015/05/14/paul-allen-just-got-one-step-clos-er-to-mapping-the-human-brain)

435. **SUPER SUPREME**

Supreme Sustenance, Sustainer, and Satisfier is G-d.

436. **MOST PERSONAL**

The Most Personal of Persons is G-d.

437. **SUPERLATIVE**

The Superlative over all superlatives is G-d.

438. **OOMPH**

The Energy of all energies is G-d.

439. **CONTINUATION**

For the person of faith, Life goes on with him or her at the time of, and after, death.

440. **BEYOND**

Life is MORE than what can be experienced through the five senses.

441. **SECRET**

The Secret to successes is Prayer.

442. **INNER SPACE**

Before I take my outer space vacation, I want to fully enjoy my Inner Space.

443. **AMENDS**

When some folks die, others try to make reparation to the deceased by doing those things they didn't do for them while they were still alive.

444. **VISION**

Some see with selfish eyes while others see with the eyes of the soul.

445. **BREATH**

Through my nose I exhale, but I inhale G-d's Breath.

446. **MANTRA'S POWER**

One's daily morning and night mantra/meditation (almost) makes one go into a G-d-like trance.

447. **POOR G-D**

Everyone continually asks Him/Her for blessings, graces, and special help. How many return the thanks that are due?

448. **G. A.**

One's Guardian Angels come in pairs.

449. **CONCEALMENT**

G-d's Camouflage/Identification is so Perfect/Unique that one can't distinguish her skin, a towel, a frying pan, or a hot, soothing cup of coffee from Him/Her.

450. **ENGINEER**

The Excellent Engineer of all engineers is G-d.

451. **EQUAL**

Our hearts should be as full of gratitude as our hands are open to receive gifts.

452. **PHARMACIST**

The Fantastic Pharmacist of all Pharmacists is G-d.

453. **REQUEST**

One shouldn't ask much of G-d—only strength and inspiration.

454. **BLESSINGS OF TRUST**

Peace and justice come with trust in G-d.

455. **IDENTITY?**

Who identifies more with one's five senses than G-d?

456. **MAGNIFICENCE**

My Magnificent Maker marvels me with His/Her multitudinous, magnanimous marvels.

457. **BREATHLESS**

The Spirit of G-d breathes in us, and we remain breathless.

458. **ESSENTIAL**

Prayer is essential because it encapsulates who we are and WHO G-D IS.

459. **PILGRIMAGE**

To consciously enter into, to embrace, one's finitude is to continue one's pilgrimage into INFINITUDE.

460. **INCOMPREHENSIBLE**

Neither proud power nor avaricious ambition can comprehend love.

461. **ART FORM**

For the Artist, everything is an art form.

462. **GREATEST**

G-d is the Greatest Good.

463. **SCULPTOR**

The Sculptor of all sculptors is G-d.

464. **COUNTENANCE**

You and I are G-d's FACE.

465. **RAPTURE**

Once in the rhythm of prayer, one doesn't want to stop.

466. **SUPER SEED**

In each of us is planted the Invisible Seed of Eternity.

467. **PRAYER'S RHYTHM**

Prayer's Rhythm resonates throughout the body, throughout the world, throughout the galaxies, and BEYOND.

468. **ABSOLUTE ART FORM**

Prayer is an Absolute Art Form.

469. **CLOSENESS**

Closer than one's breath and skin is G-d.

470. **HIGH POINT**

No beauty can surpass holiness.

471. **HABIT**

The habit of prayer must remain closer to us than our skin.

472. **RELIGIOUS HABIT?**

Some put on a religious habit but not the Habit of Prayer.

473. **GREATEST/SMALLEST**

My Greatest/Smallest Number is ONE.

474. **MIRROR**

Prayer is a mirror of our soul.

475. **EXTRA**

We are more blessed than we realize.

476. **SOLIDITY**

One can continuously repeat, "Thank you, G-d," in Bengali (*"Dhon non bad, Eshwar/Pra bhu"*) until a "permanent" synapse has been established.

477. **MATTER/NONMATTER**

Dark energy and dark matter expand, explode, and merge into the Eternal Energy/Mysterious Matter.

478. **EYE ESSENTIALS**

Food, Light, Refreshment, and Healing for one's eyes is G-d.

479. **EFFICIENCY**

Often one accomplishes more by observing the Sabbath rest than by overactivity.

480. **BRAIN**

Brainless and Brain Most is G-d.

481. **ENCOUNTER**

In experience, we find the Sacred.

482. **WORLD OXYGEN**

Prayer is the invisible, pervasive oxygen of the world.

483. **INSPIRATIONS**

The Inexhaustible, Sending Source of Inspiration is
G-d. One only needs to write the inspirations down.

484. **PRIVILEGED ART FORM**

Prayer is a privileged art form.

485. **PRAYER FORMS**

Prayer can take the form of Sublime Silence, Silence,
Silence, Silence—from a one-word to a many-word
mantra.

486. **FRANKNESS**

Prayer is openness to G-d, openness to the world's
needs, and openness to the talents of all creatures.

487. **QUALITY TIME**

We need a minimum of quality, creativity time in order to accomplish our daily, necessary tasks well.

488. **INCH**

We need to "inch up" to prayer.

489. **QUICK, POSITIVE**

Inspiration is a divine invitation. A quick, positive RSVP brings more inspiration.

490. **NEW SONG**

One needs to open one's heart and mouth and let the Lord Sing.

491. **RELAX**

To rest in Relaxing Rest is contemplative, invigorating, inspiring, and lowers one's blood pressure.

492. **MEMENTO**

Remembrance can be a powerful form of prayer, a blessing beyond compare.

493. **WEAPONRY**

One faces the lions and demons of lies with one's sharpened sword of truth, and one's long lance of love.

494. **MUSTER**

I must muster strength from the Source of All Strength.

495. **BOUNTIFUL**

To be understanding in strength, steadfast in sorrow, and resolute in the midst of slander, sarcasm, and cynicism are Bountiful Blessings indeed.

496. **POEM**

The Poem of all poems is G-d.

497. **CHANGELESS?**

Change and Changeless is G-d.

498. **G. A. G.**

Let every act be one of grace, art, and gratitude.

499. **ACUMEN**

One ought to be fascinated by the Process of Discernment because it deals directly with the Divine.

500. **ESSENTIAL QUALITIES**

Prayerful, thoughtful, joyful are three essential qualities for the Spiritual Life.

501. **CAMARADERIE**

Our Lord's Company we enjoy.

502. **TALLIT**

One's tallit becomes one's prayer tent, tabernacle, Shade in the sun, and one's Warmth in winter.

503. **IDENTICAL**

Study is prayer whether one is aware of it or not.

504. **MANTRA**

Is one's mantra's rhythm in sync with one's soul?

505. **ADSUM**

Frequently we are called by a Special Someone, but we don't answer, "*Adsum*" (Present) often enough.

506. **PANNING**
Reading and reflecting on books, magazines, and Internet sources is like panning for gold nuggets of wisdom.

507. **WHICH PATH?**
To condemn is easy. To understand, commiserate, and empathize require prayer, reflection, and contemplation.

508. **PACE**
Who doesn't need the Rhythm of Prayer to get them into the Rhythm of their Day?

509. **RHYTHM OF ONE'S DAY**
The Rhythm of one's day is G-d.

510. **HOLIDAY GIFTS**
Our gifts of prayer are wrapped with prayers of praise.

511. **LUNGFUL OF AIR**
Our Best Breath is G-d.

512. **RAIN**

Refreshing Rain is G-d.

513. **FUEL**

My fuel supply for my proverbs is meditation, contemplation, and continuous prayer of thanksgiving.

514. **OASIS**

Prayer is the Oasis in the desert of life.

515. **POUSTINIA**

Have our heart, hearth, and home become our Poustinia?

516. **PRESENCE**

The Lord's Presence is a Continuum.

517. **PERSPICACITY**

The simple/complex process of discernment refines the persons who are sincerely involved. It purifies impatience, fosters counseling, and teaches humility.

518. **BEADS**

Buddhist prayer beads bring one back to spiritual basics.

519. **PROPULSION**

One's prayer of gratitude in English can propel one into prayers of gratitude in twenty-three other languages.

520. **PRIZE**

Prayers of appreciation are the Source of proverbs and one's fuel for the day.

521. **TARGET TIME**

Right after breakfast, with hot delicious coffee in hand, is a target time for Prayer.

522. **INSCRUTABILITY**

Imperceptibly, quietly, and effectively, the Lord moves through and with us.

523. **R TO THE FOURTH**

Rest, Refuge, Recompense, and Redemption is the Lord.

524. **PENCHANT**

If one's heart is not full of G-d, then it is replete with much mud, dirt, sand, and gravel of trivialities.

525. **CONSEQUENCE**

When one gets into the Rhythm of Prayer, the Rhythm of Prayer gets into them, and their body follows suit.

526. **MAGNANIMOUS**

Every step, each breath, all conscious and subconscious acts are blessings. How indebted we are.

527. **SERAPHIC SYMPHONY**

Superb seraphic symphony is our Loveable Lord's Company.

528. **GRATEFULNESS**

May our life be a resounding "Thank you" in heaven and on earth.

529. REST IN PEACE AND AWAKE TO YOUR LORD

Oh Lord our G-d, Creator, and Consoler,
To Remember our loved one is More than a mere
matter of the mind, More than a mere matter of the
imagination.
Our Remembrance of our beloved relatives and
friends is Reality, an Engaging Encounter, a real
Spiritual Presence.
Remembering You, Oh Lord, makes You Present to us
in a Sublime, Supersensory Way.
Remembering our loved one places them and us in
the Communion of Saints,
and in Your Most Precious Presence,
Our Great, Gentle, All Gracious, All Powerful G-d.
How privileged we are. Amen.

530. IMAGINE

. . . fingertip wisdom, toenail energy, split-hair tran-
sistors, camouflaged camels, and the Invisible in the
visible.

531. TOUGHER

G-d is Stronger than anything one can say or do.

532. MINUS AND PLUS

G-d is the Least remembered by many, and the Most
Loved by a multitude.

533. PERFECT PENANCE

The unexpected penance is the most purifying and most perfect because it conforms one's unruly will to the Will of Wisdom.

534. RICHER AND RICHER

Time spent with G-d makes one richer and richer. Gold nugget proverbs are but one of numerous rewards given.

535. PRAYER'S ANSWER

One daily speaks with the Lord Who answers us with thought-provoking proverbs, and with down-to-earth suggestions for action.

536. SACRED COMMUNICATION

With one's soul, one sees you, dear deceased. Our wide-open eyes are blind to you, but our memory clearly shows us your presence.

537. ELEMENTS

Soil, sand, smoke, soot, and stars saturate the soul.

538. **NECESSITY FIRST**

Only an emergency or a pressing responsibility should take precedence over prayer. Necessity Precedes Prayer.

539. **DEATH'S BENEFIT**

The death of a beloved family member will not paralyze us, but rather increase the intensity of our spiritual life. G-d is our Spiritual Life.

540. **PURPOSE**

May all we do be for G-d's Glory and for the common good.

541. **SOURCE**

The Lord is a Treasure Trove of Proverbs and Poems.

542. **FRUITION**

May our Mighty Maker make our moments meaningful.

543. **IS**

Flexibly Inflexible is G-d.

544. GENEROSITY

Generously, gladly G-d gives gracious gifts.

545. PRAYERFUL SPIRIT

The Spirit of prayer does not come naturally nor instinctively. One must ask G-d for it, and then offer thanks every day for that gracious gift.

546. REALITY

One can't tell the difference between one's hands and G-d. One can see, feel, and sense with one's hand, and thereby knows G-d is there. Still others can believe G-d is present, but one knows G-d IS.

547. WHY WORRY?

G-d knows how and when our time, talents, and resources can be best used most efficiently.

548. SURVIVAL

Prayer is our Way to Survival.

549. MARVEL

The Super Substance of all surprising substances is our Most Moving, Uncaused Cause.

550. **HUMAN HEART HEAVEN**
Profoundly personal prayer is the uplifting upkeep,
the mesmerizing maintenance of our most beautiful
basilica, our magnificent mosque, our towering tower,
which is the human heart.

551. **ATTRIBUTES**
Fierce, ferocious, far-reaching FIRE is our G-d.

552. **LACKING**
Is one as sensitive to the promptings of the Spirit as
one should be?

553. **OPPORTUNE**
In the least expected moments, promptings of the
Spirit come. Write them down.

554. **CONCENTRATION**
. . . is prayer. One may or may not be aware of It.

555. **PRAYER**
Prayer is making a prayer our PRAYER, a word, our
WORD.

556. VACATION

One's Vacation is G-d.

557. COMPLETION

One's Strength, Sensibility, Solicitude, and Sweetness lie in Silence, Solitude, and Simplicity.

558. ACCEPTANCE

To accept one's limitations is to love oneself.

559. CATALYST

G-d is the Lightning Bolt of Truth. One is a mere firefly, a lightning rod.

560. LEARNING

Every learning adventure is Prayer.

561. ALLOWANCE

My Proverbial Master allows us to tap into His Proverb Treasure Trove.

562. REUNION

Prayer unites us with our saintly relatives, friends, and acquaintances.

563. **WISDOM**
Wisdom is the Way of Life.

564. **ABSOLUTE ACTUARY**
The Absolute Actuary of all actuaries is All-h.

565. **SUSTENANCE**
Prayer, meditation, and contemplation are the amni-
otic fluids that sustain us in G d's Womb.

566. **MON DIEU**
Oh, mon Dieu, (O, my G-d,)
Tu est Tres Grand. (You are very Great.)
Fill my soul with the past
My eyes with the present
My being with today's need.
Oh, mon Dieu.
(oui) Tu es Tres Grand.

567. **IMPACT**
Prayer cuts through verbiage.

568. **IMPRESSIONS**
Prayer stirs the soul and transforms one's being.

569. **W. W. I**

With G-d, one is "super" man; without All-h, one is
W. W. I (Weak Willie the First).

570. **OINTMENT**

Prayer is Healing Ointment that penetrates
the wounds of hate, prejudice, slights, and
misunderstandings.

571. **INSPIRATION**

Prayer is the Living Water and Font of Inspiration.

572. **LAVISH**

. . . your love on G-d and on those dearest, nearest,
and closest to you even if your Father did not lavish
his love on you.

CHAPTER TEN

PROVERBS

573. **CHOICE**

One is either a saint, a scoundrel, or a scallywag.

574. **BALANCE**

Reading negative and positive stuff at a ratio of eight to one is like having more sodium than potassium in one's system.

575. **HUMILITY**

Share the glory and the gain; share the shame and the pain.

576. **OUTCOME**

When the Spirit of St. Francis of Assisi is thrown aside, trials, troubles, and crimes multiply.

577. **NAME CHANGE**

Innocent III should be more aptly called Bellicus Deceptus III or Machiavellius II.

578. **BELIEF**

. . . is an eternal life insurance policy.

579. DEATH

. . . is the most maligned and feared member of the human family.

580. EQUALIZER

The prospect of death of a loved one brings tears to the eyes of even the toughest amongst us.

581. ALTERNATIVE

Better to build strong, informed, holy leaders than to construct big, beautiful buildings.

582. ANOTHER PARADOX

We are delicately strong, tender, and tough creatures.

583. SELECTION

Love or self-interest. Which?

584. BLAME

If the devil is behind the sexual abuse of children and women, then a leading church official must be the devil.

585. **DEMOCRACY'S ENEMIES**

Powermongers are enemies of democracy.

586. **ADDICTION**

If religion is the opium of the people, then power-mongering is heroin.

587. **SELECT**

Some actions have a price; others have value.

588. **AMAZEMENT**

Who is the archbishop who has beautiful cardinals coming to his backyard?

589. **MULTINATIONAL**

I am Putam (Beloved) of Punjab; Tashi (Peace) of the ravaged monasteries of Tibet; Pinchas Ahili (Patrick Ernest) of Massacre Street, Tel Aviv; Tariq Ibn Ziyad of ancient Morocco; Murph the Irish bullfighter; and Brave Eagle of the Shoshone-Arapahoe nation.

590. **DAVID REVISITED**

Truth's well-chosen stones will topple the Goliaths of corruption.

591. TIREDNESS

. . . speaks out of turn and gets one into terrible trouble.

592. WHICH?

Between anger and determination, a threadbare line exists.

593. TRULY?

The people of Hoboken, New Jersey, speak Hobokenese.

594. SENSITIVITY

Disagreement does not mean disloyalty.

595. WIRY

One may be old, but one is not decrepit . . . yet.

596. LEADERSHIP

A leader's vocation is to form as many leaders as possible until his own vocation becomes extinct.

597. **TOO MANY**

. . . beautiful buildings are often staffed by ugly people.

598. **OHHH?**

One can be slow, certain, and yet be somewhat sophisticated.

599. **PROSPECTING**

G-d's messages are gold nuggets hidden beneath a heap of verbiage.

600. **PRECISION**

Church denotes dignity, decorum, and trustworthiness. *Institution* is cold even in summer.

601. **SEMANTICS**

Penance and conversion, not structural change simply means some of the hierarchy are accountable to no one.

602. **ARCHANGEL OF CLEANLINESS**

One can consistently clean up clutter.

603. **ILLUSION**

To live an illusion is to have one's inner core corrupted and contaminated.

604. **AFTEREFFECT**

David took a stone and brought down a mighty man.

605. **RICHES**

To be rich in vocabulary and in virtue is to be rich indeed.

606. **CONSISTENCY**

. . . accomplishes more than mere intelligence.

607. **THE INQUISITION**

. . . is still alive and kicking the hell out of us.

608. **POSSIBILITY**

During homeroom, one of Trujillo's seven-grade students with her homework in hand asked him, "Which is the bigger sex organ: the liver or the heart?"

"Good question," he answered just as the bell for first class rang.

609. **RELIABILITY**

Some folks are as reliable as wonderful winter weather in Winnebago, Wisconsin.

610. **QUIRK OF FATE**

When temperatures fall below zero Fahrenheit, it's hard to believe in global warming.

611. **PRECAUTION**

Sickness and solitude don't go well together.

612. **KIND FLOWER**

An orchid of kindness while one is alive is more precious than a bouquet of roses when she is dead.

613. **RICH MAN/POOR MAN**

One is and is not rich in terms of time.

614. **PRICE OF PEACE**

What hell St. Francis of Assisi had to endure to bring G-d's message of Peace.

615. **TRIOS**

Loving kindness, mercy, and graciousness are triplets.

616. DICTATORIAL ATTIRE
Not all dictators are civil.

617. ATHEISM'S PURPOSE
. . . is to refine the believer's Belief.

618. LOVE'S ZENITH
Kabbalists, Buddhist monks, Sufi holy men and women, and Christian mystics have one common goal: intense love of the Mysterious.

619. TENSION
To live with hate is to live in a constant/continuous state of tension.

620. INDISPENSABLE
Correction is like water; however, no one needs a terrifying Tsunami.

621. HUMMM
Some folks are so sick they go to the pharmacy in their colorful, and their not-so-colorful, pajamas.

622. **MERCIFUL MAN**

. . . is a title that outranks all others.

623. **SECRECY**

. . . is hidden agenda.

624. **MOCKERY**

Some folks are not good enough to be included in an important event, but they are good enough persons from whom membership dues and donations are received. The "not good enough" have become the whipping boys upon whom the anger, frustration, and rage against an institution are vented.

625. **FOURSOME**

Peace, reconciliation, completion, and forbearance are quadruplets.

626. **POVERTY OF SPIRIT**

The poor in spirit are expected to do much with few resources.

627. **ATHEISTS' FATE**
The atheist can look forward to an "ultimate cold death of Nothingness."
(See E. Sahtouris, quoted in Donald J. Prose, "Science and Theology Meet Again," p. 3)

628. **DETERMINATION**
One is more determined than one looks.

629. **LAST NAME**
When someone's new last name is Quished (a Siberian-Irish mixture?), then his new first name must be Distin.

630. **TWO-SIDED EXPERIENCE**
Too many have experienced the beauty of the Bahamas, the calm of the Caribbean, and the terror of torture.

631. **HEDONISTS**
Some are work-happy hedonists.

632. **LIVING PEACE**

When you meet a delightful man whose name is Rishi, who speaks Hindi, and whose Muslim wife's name is Bibi, please tell him, "I know of a man whose Tibetan name is Tashi (Peace), and the two of you are living Mahatma Gandhi's dream of peace."

633. **PROVIDENCE**

When things are going bad for you, G-d will send you a Jew . . . like me. When life for you looks grim, All-h will send you a Muslim . . . like me. When you can't take life anymore as a Protestant, G-d will send you a Catholic gallant . . . like me. When you've lost your most precious amethyst, the Living One will send you a Buddhist . . . like me. When life gets boring as a vegetarian, G-d will send you a Unitarian . . . like me.

634. **PLEASANT SURPRISE**

In Jersey City, New Jersey, have you seen the following Indian name, which sounds Irish: Deepak O. Shah, who is an MD, FACC?

635. **FAMILY**

Those who live a good life are brothers and sisters of Goodness.

636. **LIFELESS**

Have you ever removed your comfortable, beige knee-stitched Bermuda shorts with as much energy as a flopping, gasping minnow on a sunbaked rock?

637. **MY . . . MY**

Her buttocks, like two over-stuffed pillows, bulged out of her gray sweat pants.

638. **SHOCK**

Her breasts hung down like two long pieces of string dangling from a living skeleton.

639. **AUTHENTICITY**

History, presented by reputable historians, is distinctly and refreshingly distinct from that written, and given the *imprimatur* ("Let it be printed") and the *nihil obstat* ("There is no obstacle").

640. **SECOND MIRACLE**

If a church dignitary truly repented, then the second miracle needed for a saint was at hand.

641. **UPRIGHTNESS**

To die a worthy death, one must pay his moral debt.

642. **POSITION**

During World War II, there were those who were pro-Nazi, those who were anti-Nazi, and those who were neutral. Today, there are those who are papists, those who are anti-papists, and those who are neutral.

643. **SHORT SHORTS**

If a teenager's short shorts covered her buttocks like her brown cowboy boots covered her up to her ankles, then she'd be well dressed.

644. **IMMOBILIZATION**

Many organizations/institutions remain immobilized by their hate-love relationship with authority.

645. **CONTRADICTION**

Some institutions equate real Saints with criminals.

646. **VINCIBLE IGNORANCE**

Those who persist in working for church reform from within not only suffer from "battered spouse syndrome," but also are in an almost incurable state of denial.

647. **SIMONY**

To see a notable church official, attend his Mass, and receive his blessing for much, much money causes some to see this as high-class simony.

648. **CAUTION**

Beware of those who are more theologians than historians.

649. **EQUILIBRIUM**

The more one receives massive amounts of information, the more one needs contemplation in order to make balanced evaluations.

650. **PERFECTION**

Some folks are so perfect they never get angry at those who get angry with one of their family members.

651. **APPEARANCES**

Some remarks are as elegant as the cheap paper on which they are written.

652. **ANESTHESIA**

Many have become anesthetized to the crimes of the home.

653. **METAMORPHOSIS**

If one used to look upon agnostics, atheists, and those who belittled and scorned religion as religious bullies, then delving into history can make one more compassionate toward them.

654. **APPEARANCE**

To be "refined" on the outside but coarse on the inside is like a sanitized but infected gold-ring-snouted hog.

655. **"ISMS" PLAGUE**

Many institutions are plagued by Manicheanism, Stoicism, and Pelagianism.

656. **NEGLECT**

Negligence is the scourge of government and religion.

657. **TONGUE-TIED**

Would commercial producers become tongue-tied if they stopped using *presenting* and *introducing* ad nauseam in their sales pitches?

658. SHOULD

Should is a talk-the-talk tidbit, a mournful "mouther," a boastful self-touter, a neurotic nobody, a wistful willy-nilly, a platonic player, a play-it-safe Sandie, an inactive belly button blunder.

659. PIETISM

Too many of our people have rotten education teeth because their eating habits do not include a historically accurate meat/fish/poultry, potatoes, vegetable, and fruit diet.

660. IMPERFECT

Some are attractive in all aspects except for their breath—a combination of horrible garlic, horseradish, Limburger cheese, and purple onion.

661. IMPROVEMENT

Does one's writing and second language improve with anger?

662. TIT FOR TAT

If insurance companies were as quick to save money for the consumer as they are to deny legitimate health claims, all would bow their heads in respect.

663. **OBITUARY**

In planning one's funeral, the following should be considered:

- Short, personalized prayers by one's spouse and family members
- A Hebrew and Muslim Blessing
- A polka finale
- And a fiesta and dancing following the service.

664. **HOLY SEX**

Are condoms blessed by someone in sacred orders holy sex?

665. **SAVVY**

Some folks don't know the difference between collegial action and a mandated directive.

666. **CONSEQUENCES**

To live unjustly is to die in disgrace.

667. **IMPOSSIBLE**

How can one win when being good is equated with being a homosexual, when being a heterosexual is interpreted as being a libertine, and when one helps the poor, he is libeled/labeled a Communist?

668. **RUPTURE**

The international sex abuse scandal is a rupture in society's armor.

669. **DECLARATION OF DEPENDENCE?**

Has our country become a government of politicians, for politicians, and by politicians?

670. **MODEL**

If the prime exemplar is wanting in virtue, then no small wonder when lesser mortals follow suit.

671. **PROPORTIONALITY**

The more others hoard money, the more we will give where it is needed.

672. **SUPREME HONOR**

A priest walked into the nurse superintendent's office and said, "You honor me more than all the other ministers and rabbis."

"What are you talking about?" she answered.

"On the second floor at the entrance of the obstetrics and gynecology department, a sign above the door reads Father's Waiting Room."

673. **UNIQUE ARCHITECTURE**
The human body is the most delicately designed, most detailed, and devoutly blessed, superbly sustained, and intricately created micro/macrocosm.

674. **DAMNATIONS**
Dogmatic damnations fall on the deaf, the dead, and the daring.

675. **ADMONITION**
Better the way of the wise than the perverse path of the powerful.

676. **ARCHEOLOGY**
The story of stones is written by the wind, water, the sands of time, and the hand of man.

677. **DIFFERENCE**
What a difference there is between a mystery and a contradiction.

678. **WEAPONS OF CHOICE**
Blame, scorn, and derision have for centuries been the weapons of choice in psychological warfare against innocent victims.

679. DISINFORMATION

Some institutions thrive on disinformation, and then attribute their success to the Holy Spirit. Shame.

680. RAYS OF HOPE

History, science, and good example scatter the darkness of ignorance.

681. PRICELESS

Is the most valuable part of oneself the gold crown in one's mouth?

682. RECONSIDER

Why do the poor have to pay for the expensive trips of a rich man?

683. ENTITLEMENT

Some would be better called "Promoters of Immorality" than "Defenders of the Faith."

684. INCREDIBILITY

Do institutions that specialize in condemnations deserve to be called holy?

685. **THIS OR THAT**

Some fulfill themselves and edify mankind while others debase themselves and defile the unsuspecting.

686. **DISPENSATION**

Dispensation from vowed celibacy is like the Communist Rehabilitation Program for Cuban Political Prisoners of Conscience—both require one's signature, which attests to a lie.

687. **"SAINT" JEROME**

Is Jerome the Patron Saint of Manicheans, Stoics, Scriptural Errancy, and anti-Semitism?

688. **"SAINT" AUGUSTINE**

Is Augustine the Patron Saint of libertines, misogynists, and Original Sin?

689. **EYEFUL**

Are we so accustomed to looking with our eyes that we forget or neglect to penetrate the periphery?

690. **EXEMPLARS**

Those who pose as the moral guardians of the world should themselves be steeped in history and universal values and principles.

691. **GUARD OR GUARDIAN?**

What a difference between a Guardian and a paid guard of the Sacraments.

692. **APPENDAGE**

Certain individuals should have the following letters added to their surname: BBB (Bullyboy of the Barrio), HRV (Human Rights Violator), and DRO (Divine Right Oppressor).

693. **EXPECTANCY**

Seven stacks of paperwork wait like a pack of hungry hyenas.

694. **INSENSITIVITY**

Let us not become anesthetized to crime.

695. **BONDING**

Sincerity, openness, and mutual support result in a bonding that comes from the heart.

696. **DESIRE**
Those who wish to be saints should start early.

697. **USELESS**
Amazing indeed how a multitude of prayers offered for one person have not made them better. In fact, they are worse.

698. **MEMORIAL**
Multiple memories mingle in my mind and make me smile.

699. **POPE ALEXANDER VI**
While he was still cardinal, Rodrigo Borgia had three children. After he became pope, Alexander VI had six more children. Is he the Patron Saint of (un)married priests?
(See Sarah Bradford, *Lucrezia Borgia*, pp. xvi–xvii.)

700. **EMPTINESS**
Empty heart, empty mind, empty hands.

701. **EQUALITY**
Who should care what color a person is: black, white, yellow, brown, or green. They are still a human being.

702. **WELL GROOMED**

One may be old like his boots, but he's clean and highly polished.

703. **CD HEAVEN**

Who wouldn't be in quintessential heaven when thirteen interlinear Hebrew/English CD translations of the Bible arrive?

704. **DRIVEN?**

Mission-driven or money-driven? Which is the better over-drive?

705. **EVEN COUPLE**

Science clarifies. Faith solidifies.

706. **E. H.**

Too many folks are E. H. (e-mail homeless).

707. **CREATIVITY**

Rest, tranquility, and the quest for truth are the fountains of creativity.

708. **STATION**

Some are vowed celibates, others are married priests, and some are somewhere in between.

709. **INFECTION**

Ingratitude, like an infection, spreads from parent to child.

710. **MASTER KEY**

Adaptability is the master key to success.

711. **OUTRAGEOUS**

Does a schismatic collaborator dare to call the innocent criminals?

712. **TOLERANCE**

To be fruitful, the multiple paths of tolerance must first be trod.

713. **DOUBT**

Sometimes one doesn't know where selfishness ends and prudence begins.

714. **UNEXPECTED CREATIVITY**

If one does his/her best to enjoy even the dullest, even the most mundane of activities, then inspiration will come unexpectedly.

715. **SURPRISE VISIT**

Inspiration is a surprise visit from G-d and/or from the Archangel Gabriel.

716. **BETTER MODE**

Instead of choosing the lesser of two evils, why not select the better of two options?

717. **TREASURE OR ENIGMA**

Some events are memorable; others live on in disgrace.

718. **ME**

Who is not frail, mortal, and limited in many ways?

719. **POSSIBLE PEACE**

When all science leaders and all religious leaders critically examine their own historical roots, then peace is possible.

720. **COMMONALITY**

History is the thread that comprises mankind's garment.

721. **NEW FACE**

A collegial and coresponsible face must replace the stern, authoritarian, and totalitarian type.

722. **HUMBLENESS**

To get help in using a bedpan is one of the greatest aids in acquiring humility.

723. **DOUBLE HUMM**

How many cousins tell you, "You speak Spanish with an Irish accent"?

724. **HUMOR**

One of the best times for humor is when events are deadly serious.

725. **E. C. E.**

I am a member of the Exclusive Club of the *Excommunicandi.*

726. **B. A. A. & P. I. B.**

The following need to be added to my last name: B. A. A. (Brother Ass Archbishop), and P. I. B. (Pain in the Butt).

727. **STOP**

To see who punishes success and rewards failure, one need look no further than the Adriatic Sea.

728. **LITANY OF SAINTS REVISED**

Certain names need to be removed while others must be added to the Litany of Saints.

729. **SUBLIME SYNTAX**

G-d is the Present Participle of all verbs, the Absolute Adjective of all adjectives.

730. **DIALOGUE OF THE DEAF**

(attributed to Cardinal William Levada)
This seems to mean: "Listen to the Vatican," while the Vatican does not have to listen to anyone.
(See http://ncronline.org/blogs/ncr-today/ vatican-official-warns-dialogue-deaf-lcwr)

731. **FREEDOM**

Some folks talk freedom but intend coercion, domination, and monopoly.

732. **DISPARITY**

Does one complain more than one thanks G-d?

733. **BLENDING**

There ought not be any disconnect or divorce between sexuality and spirituality.

734. **TEACHER RECRUITMENT**

Why can't we recruit our teachers from the top 10 percent of universities and colleges?

735. **SYMBOLS?**

Does the scarlet sash stand for the victims' blood of ages past? Does the magenta beanie represent scarlet-red character assassination by those in power?

736. **NECESSITY VS. SIN**

Necessity negates sin.

737. ANONYMOUS ENEMY

An institution that hides behind its money, its political clout, and its anonymity is an enemy of mankind.

738. SCARF, STOLE, TALLIT

Who has the experience of tossing his tallit helter-skelter into the dryer with the rest of washed and rinsed clothes, and then having it always come out folded lengthwise like a scarf or a stole?

739. CRIMINALITY

Some try to deflect their own criminality by libeling/labeling others criminals.

740. SECULARISM'S ENIGMA

If the accumulation of great wealth is a sign of secularism, then certain institutions rank among the most secular.

741. FRATERNAL TWINS

For some, there is no difference between totalitarianism and freedom.

742. **GRACE AND BEAUTY**

"Beauty without grace becomes invisible, but grace without beauty can still charm."
(Will & Ariel Durant, *The Age of Voltaire*, p. 8)

743. **MANNERS**

"Good manners are of the mind as well as of the body, and both kinds will be influenced by the company we keep."
(Will & Ariel Durant, *The Age of Voltaire*, p. 8)

744. **IDEAS**

"All ideas are ultimately derived from experience through impressions."
(Will & Ariel Durant, *The Age of Voltaire*, p. 14)

745. **LABOR**

"Everything in the world is purchased by labor."
(Will & Ariel Durant, *The Age of Voltaire*, p. 15)

746. **MISTRESS OF WISDOM**

History is "the great mistress of wisdom."
(Will & Ariel Durant, *The Age of Voltaire*, p. 156, quoted from Mosner's *Hume*, p. 31)

747. **DIET**

Too many have been given a cake-candy-and-ice-cream diet of piety, and no meat-fish-vegetables-and-fruit diet of history.

748. **FRIENDSHIP REFINED**

"Friendship is the chief joy of human life," said David Hume.

(Will & Ariel Durant, *The Age of Voltaire*, p. 159, quoted from David Hume's *My Own Life: Dialogues Concerning Natural Religions*, p. 23)

749. **NOBILITY**

"A tree," said Alexander Pope, "is a nobler object than a prince in his coronation robes."

(Will & Ariel Durant, *The Age of Voltaire*, p. 169, quoted from J. C. Thompson, *Table Talk from Ben Johnson to Leigh Hunt*, p. 11)

750. **GRACIOUS GRATITUDE**

"Let us be grateful that our reason is limited and our future unknown."

(Will & Ariel Durant, *The Age of Voltaire*, p. 17)

751. **STABILITY**

One needs just enough rest to heal and just enough exercise to make one strong.

752. **WHITEWASH**

To belittle history is to whitewash evil.

753. **TRASH**

Theology without a historical basis is trash.

754. **QUID PRO QUO (TIT FOR TAT)**

"Knowledge implements vice as much as it enlightens morality."
(Will & Ariel Durant, *The Age of Voltaire*, p. 33)

755. **CLARITY**

"Clearness is the ornament of deep thought."
(Will & Ariel Durant, *The Age of Voltaire*, p. 338, taken from Luc de Clapiers, Marquis de Venargues, *Oeuvres Choisies*, CXV, IX)

756. **EMOTIONAL QUOTIENT**

"Perhaps we owe to the passions the greatest accomplishments of the intellect . . ."
(Will & Ariel Durant, *The Age of Voltaire*, p. 339, taken from Venargues, *Oeuvres Choises*, CL.)

757. **TEMPORARY CONQUEST**

Evil example often overpowers one's belief in G-d.

758. **TAKE HEED**

When the guinea pig becomes a wild boar, let meddlers beware.

759. **KNOWLEDGE**

G-d's knowledge of us is much more intimate, profound, and insightful than that of parents who know their own children.

760. **ACCIDENT?**

Did you know a wagon pulled by a horse and involved in an accident was called a "miscarriage"?

761. **TWO TITLES**

Two titles have been added to a certain bishop's repertoire: Monseigneur l'Eveque Unpeud'eau (the Watery Bishop) and Le Fou de Foix (The Fool of Foix, France).

762. **VENDETTA**

Some institutions have vendetta deeply imbedded in their DNA.

763. **CHALLENGE**

"You are never so divine as when you lead us through pleasure to wisdom and truth."
(Will & Ariel Durant, *The Age of Voltaire*, p. 34)

764. **CLIMATE'S INFLUENCE**

"In a word, climate is the first, and at first the most powerful factor in determining a people's economy, its laws, and its 'national character.'"
(Will & Ariel Durant, *The Age of Voltaire*, p. 34)

765. **PRUDENCE**

"We must move slowly in trying to change a custom."
(Will & Ariel Durant, *The Age of Voltaire*, p. 35)

766. **CHOOSE**

Should we be building more buildings or constructing more communities?

767. **BEST NAME**

Does it matter if, to some, one is considered a heretic, a criminal; to others, an infidel; and to still others, a radical as long as one's spouse calls one Beloved Darling?

768. **CHECKS AND BALANCES**

"State and Church should act as checks and balances to each other, but should always remain separate; 'this great distinction [is] the basis of the tranquility of nations.'"
(Will & Ariel Durant, *The Age of Voltaire*, p. 355; taken from George Havens, *The Age of Ideas*, p. 12)

769. **FOUR HALLMARKS**

Pretty, petty, prominent, and pagan characterize too many.

770. **EXQUISITE GIFT**

"Reason is the most perfect, the most noble, the most beautiful of all our faculties." *(Le raison est le plus parfait, le plus noble, et le plus exquis de tous les sens.)* (Will & Ariel Durant, *The Age of Voltaire*, p. 356; taken from Emile Faguet, *Dix-huitieme siècle: Etudes littéraires, Paris; Literary History of France*, New York, 1907, p. 19)

771. **EMOTIONAL CAUSE**

"Study has been for me the sovereign remedy against all disappointments of life. I have never known any trouble that an hour's reading would not dissipate." (Will & Ariel Durant, *The Age of Voltaire*, p. 359; taken from Charles de Secondat, Baron de Montesquieu, in F. J. Hearnshaw, *Social and Political Ideas of Some Great French Thinkers of the Age of Reason*, p. 11)

772. **HOUSEWIFE'S HORROR**

What can be more distressful than black ink splotched from a black pen on clean white clothes freshly taken from the dryer?

773. **BIGHEARTEDNESS**

Generosity serves the giver well.

774. FAME/INFAMY

Some are better known for their indoctrination than for their works of charity.

775. ADVENTURE PAR EXCELLENCE

The future is the grandest of all adventures.

776. RUSH TO . . .

Some rush to save seconds but waste days, months, years, and opportunities.

777. SYMPATHY'S SYMPHONY

My soul sings a symphony of sympathy for spouses separated and saturated with sorrow.

778. LOVE TO ROSITA

Robust rhapsodies ring roses around Rosita Samires.

779. LOVE'S YEARNING

Love's languor languishes and loses longevity while lavishing long-lasting lachrymose love songs in latent lavender laurels.

780. **PREJUDICE'S POSTURE**

Prejudice hides its porcupine posture in its hideous heart and in well-planned phrases.

781. **SCOURGE**

Negligence is the scourge of family life, education, business, government, religion, medical practice, and politics.

782. **TIP-TOP SHAPE**

Who has had two catheterizations and four stents, has developed atrial fibrillation (irregular heartbeat), vomited about thirty-two times in a two-month period from allergic reactions to medicine, then says, "Outside of that, I'm fine"?

783. **DUAL MEMBERSHIP**

Dual membership is held by many: one in an institution, the other in a church.

784. **LOVE OF SELF**

Love of self comes before love of others.

785. **BETTER**

Knowledge is both a help and a hindrance. Wisdom makes the difference.

786. **TEETER-TOTTER**

"Tranquility is a fine thing but ennui . . . belongs to the same family."
(Will & Ariel Durant, *The Age of Voltaire*, p. 473; taken from John Morley, *Life of Voltaire*, p. 20)

787. **CEREBELLUM?**

A very intelligent female student calls herself Sarah Bellum.

788. **WASTE**

One form of waste leads to another.

789. **ALAS**

"Woe to those who liberate hatred but chain the mind."
(Will & Ariel Durant, *The Age of Voltaire*, p. 47)

790. **PARADIGMS**

Society needs many models of industry, sobriety, unity, and thrift.

(See Will & Ariel Durant, *The Age of Voltaire*, p. 47)

791. **WISDOM'S MISTRESS**

David Hume called history "the great mistress of wisdom."

(See Will & Ariel Durant, *The Age of Voltaire*, p. 15)

792. **WHISTLE-BLOWERS**

Ecclesiastical whistle-blowers are treated as badly as or worse than secular ones.

793. **CONFUCIUS**

"The *espirits forts* rejoiced to find that Confucius was a free thinker rather than a displaced Jesuit."

(Will & Ariel Durant, *The Age of Voltaire*, p. 50)

794. **ABSOLUTE REPOSE**

"Death is the absolute repose of the body."

(Will & Ariel Durant, *The Age of Voltaire*, p. 51)

795. **FATIGUE**

An emotional assault is more wearisome than strenuous physical activity.

796. **LIMITATIONS?**

One's limitations are often blessings in disguise.

797. **CHEMISTRY'S PURPOSE**

"The object and chief business of chemistry is skillfully to separate substances into their constituents, to discover their properties, and to compound them in different ways."
(Will & Ariel Durant, *The Age of Voltaire*, p. 525, taken from Karl Wilhelm Scheele, *Treatise on Fire and Air*, in A. Wolf, *History of Science, Technology, and Philosophy in the Eighteenth Century*, p. 35)

798. **SOUR MILK'S ACIDITY**

Karl Wilhelm Scheele proved that "the acidity of sour milk is due to lactic acid."
(See Will & Ariel Durant, *The Age of Voltaire*, p. 52)

799. **HONEYPOURS**

Those who eat honey from the local area only are honeypours.

800. **LEVEL VARIATIONS**
The CEO of VC has a job, the reds have careers, and the rest of us have vocations.

801. **LIFE RECORD**
Blood pressure numbers are the alphabet with which G-d writes one's life.

802. **DISTINGUISH**
Whether someone has a particular talent but never uses it is difficult to ascertain. Perhaps, one never had it to begin with.

803. **G-DLIKE**
The persecuted of the ghettos and the catacombs are more G-dlike than the followers of Constantine.

804. **HIGH-CLASS COMPANY**
Today, a black baby and a white baby Mercedes-Benz, "sons" of a patriarch Mercedes Brilliant Metallic Gray E350 4Matic GLK-SUV and a matriarch Mercedes S350 Beige Crème Cabriolet, passed someone in his humble 2008 white Ford Fusion.

805. **TENACITY**
Some hold on to life by a Timeless, Thorough Thread; others possess the full, Beautiful Garment of Life, but die suddenly and unexpectedly.

806. **ALTERNATIVE MEDICINE**
If one ever gets cancer or benign tumors or polyps, should one consider taking massive doses (twenty-three capsules) of shark cartilage daily from a reputable source before submitting to surgery, chemotherapy, or radiation therapy?

807. **PERCEPTION**
An institution that excoriates, excommunicates, condemns, defames, and slanders is hardly in a position to form leaders of integrity.

808. **LESSER OF TWO**
One may be forgotten, but at least one doesn't have to live and die in disgrace.

809. **PROCLIVITY**
Whether one lives in a prison or in a monk's cell, one can live a fruitful, creative life, or endure a time-wasted existence.

810. **EMOTION OWNERSHIP**

Owning one's emotions is the first of many creative steps.

811. **BULLIES**

Bullies push their weight around with their muscle, their might, and their money.

812. **PROOF**

Evidence exists for work well done and for negligence.

813. **FAÇADES**

Too many hide behind religiosity, formality, and aloofness.

814. **PROPELLING POWER**

Pride propels for good or evil.

815. **OBEDIENCE**

One's spouse should blindly obey only one command: "Eat it while it's hot."

816. TWO TYPES

Nostalgic foot draggers coexist with dynamic, cosmic catalysts, power-hungry institutional traditionalists, and with Vatican II advocates.

817. KILLING

Character, literary, and verbal assassination are only one step behind homicide.

818. LOOKING GLASS

How dare someone call a theologian's work or opus "dangerous and deviant" when he himself fits that description!

819. GIFT UNUSUAL

To expect the Unexpected is an Unusual Gift.

820. HALFHEARTED

Betimes, one is considered worthy of consideration, but not always deemed worthy of other's time, talent, and moral support.

821. SHORTSIGHTED

Sometimes complex issues have a simple solution.

822. **BIG THREE**

Clarity, Charity, Integrity. What more do we need?

823. **INEXPLICABLE**

Violence and murder cannot adequately be explained
. . . Only empathy, sharing, and prayer help.

824. **HISTORY'S PRICE**

Delving into history can get you in trouble with certain institutions.

825. **BLEMISH REMOVAL**

Getting rid of lies is like removing indelible ink from
a silk garment—dedicated elbow grease and scientific
know-how become solutions.

826. **WARNING**

Beware of the sanitized robed one who carries venom
in his veins.

827. **DISCREPANCY**

If as much effort and money were spent helping the
poor as is done castigating, denigrating, and belittling
those who do good, what a better world 'twould be.

828.   **FAIR DEALING**
Obedience is fine as long as the dictator remains benevolent.

829.   **PREPOSTEROUS**
Can you imagine paying $3 million to have yourself or your "kith and kin" investigated?

830.   **TRANSPARENCY**
Freedom, creativity, and openness are anathema to those in power.

831.   **PROPORTION**
Hans Kung has said, "One priest is nobody. Ten priests are a threat taken seriously, fifty priests are invincible."
("Kung Still Resists the 'Roman Inquisition,'" *National Catholic Reporter*, January 4–17, 2012, p.)

832.   **MULTIPLE CLEAN BIRTHDAYS**
In a year, someone will have sung "Happy Birthday to Me" 7,300 times while he washes his hands. Only Sanjay Gupta, MD, sings it more than him.

833. **SUPPOSE**

If those who call themselves holy were as their name purports to be, what a blessed world 'twould be.

834. **ABSTRACTION**

Is abstract thought really abstract, or is it more real than we realize?

835. **PAR EXCELLENCE**

To be consumed by one's thoughts is to be a mystic, philosopher, mathematician, physicist, scientist, writer, poet, etc., or a combination of the above; in a word, to be excellent in one's field(s).

836. **BRIDGES**

Geniuses are the bridges between the Genius and ourselves.

837. **EXCLUSIVE CLUB**

Have you ever called a friend and said, "Let me be the first to welcome you into the exclusive club of the *excommunicandi*" (the excommunicated)?

838. **TOUCHET A VOUS**

"Radical feminist themes incompatible with
the Catholic faith," the Vatican's critique of the
Conference of Women Religious, would be better phrased: "Practical, logical, historical feminine
standards incompatible with ole boys sexist club
mentality."
(See Clare Malone, "Holy Rollers, Nuns on the Bus,"
p. 27)

839. **BEING PRECEDES ACTION**

A person tends to treat others the way one is.

840. **B TO THE SEVENTH POWER**

Don't a lot of folks have a wife who is called Babe,
Beautiful, Bounteous, Barbie, Black-and-Blue Honey-
Bunch? Hasn't she fallen only forty times since 2007,
when she had her stroke?

841. **OPIUM**

If religion is the "opium of the people," then meticu-
lously measure the amount.

(See http://en.wikipedia.org/wiki/Opium_of_the_
people. The phrase "This opium you feed your people" appeared in 1797 in Marquis de Sade's text and
Novalis's "[R]eligion acts merely as an opiate" around
the same time. The full quote from Karl Marx is:
"Religion is the sigh of the oppressed creature, the
heart of a heartless world, and the soul of soulless
conditions. It is the opium of the people." Often
quoted, the interpretation of the metaphor in its context has received much less attention.)

842. **SWENCH**

Whoever mixes Swedish with French speaks *Swench*.

843. **TAGALISH**

Whoever mixes Tagalog with English speaks *Tagalish*.

844. **CHINFIN/FINNESE**

Whoever combines Chinese with Finnish communicates in *Chinfin* or *Finnese*.

845. **ARABESE**

One who blends Arabic with Chinese speaks *Arabese*.

846. **SWEDIC**

Whoever combines Arabic with Swedish communicates in *Swedic*.

847. **SPANDARIN**

She who expresses herself simultaneously in Spanish and Mandarin uses *Spandarin*.

848. **HINDESE**

She who combines Hindi with Chinese speaks *Hindese*.

849. **PORTAGARIN**

Whoever expresses himself in the same sentence in both Portuguese and Mandarin uses *Portagarin*.

850. **BENGALESE**

He who combines Bengali with Chinese communicates in *Bengalese*.

851. **BENGALIAN**

Whoever mixes Bengali with Russian speaks *Bengalian*.

852. **PUNJABESE**

She who uses both Punjabi and Japanese speaks *Punjabese.*

853. **CHINJABI/ PUNCHIN**

He who mixes Punjabi with Chinese speaks *Chinjabi or Punchin.*

854. **GERGALI**

She who mixes German with Bengali speaks *Gergali.*

855. **KORENCH**

He who mixes Korean with French speaks *Korench.*

856. **URDARATI**

Whoever mixes Urdu with Gujarati speaks *Urdarati.*

857. **POLISIAN**

One who mixes Persian with Polish speaks *Polisian.*

858. **MALAPANESE**

Whoever mixes Malayalam with Japanese speaks *Malapanese.*

859. **TAGALAKRANIAN**

He who mixes Tagalog with Ukrainian speaks *Tagalakrainian*.

860. **ROMANUTCH**

She who mixes Romanian with Dutch speaks *Romanutch*.

861. **SOMALABIC**

Whoever mixes Somali with Arabic speaks *Somalabic*.

862. **HUNGARISH**

He who mixes Hungarian with English speaks *Hungarish*.

863. **CZECHISH**

One who mixes Czech with English speaks *Czechish*.

864. **PASHTALIAN**

Whoever mixes Pashto and Italian speaks *Pashtalian*.

865. **DUTCHALIAN**

He who mixes Dutch with Italian speaks *Dutchalian*.

866. **GREEKINESE**

Whoever mixes Greek with Chinese speaks *Greekinese.*

867. **HUNGARATALAN**

She who mixes Hungarian with Catalan speaks *Hungaratalan.*

868. **BULGARIABIC**

One who mixes Bulgarian with Arabic speaks *Bulgariabic.*

869. **SWETALIAN**

Whoever mixes Swedish with Italian speaks *Swetalian.*

870. **FRENISH**

She who mixes French with English speaks *Frenish.*

871. **ARMENISH**

One who mixes Armenian with English speaks *Armenish.*

872. **EVANGELIZATION?**

How dare an institution evangelize others when it should evangelize its own leaders first.

873. **INSUFFERABLE**

To expect a man to live a life of vowed celibacy is like expecting him to shut down his own libido.

874. **ECUMENICAL SPIRIT**

A simple hymn/song/chant translated into another language can convey the Spirit of Ecumenism.

875. **CHOICES**

There exist pastors and hatchet men.

876. **TRUE DEPENDENCE**

One's spiritual sons and daughters have become more and more dependent on G-d and themselves; less and less dependent on their spiritual father. Good.

877. **MORE THAN THOU**

There are those who are more saintly than thou, stronger than thou, wealthier than thou, and more snobbish than thou.

878. **UNPRETENTIOUSNESS**

To undergo a biopsy is to realize one's dependency on G-d or to submit to a sense of despair.

879. **TRUE TREASURE**

What good is it to have money, power, and real estate but lack morals?

880. **ANALOGOUS UNIVERSE**

Is the human brain an archetype of the universe(s), or is the universe an archetype of the human brain?

881. **TRANSFORMATION**

To channel anger to a creative purpose is no small feat.

882. **CANONIZATION?**

Canonization is no guarantee of sanctity, neither of the canonized nor of the one(s) who forward(s) the cause.

883. **BATTLES**

Some fight big battles with the big boys; others fight their biggest battles with themselves.

884. ANNOYANCE

Those who think their way is the best are disgruntled by those who disagree with them.

885. FORETHOUGHT

To make the right choice at the right time is prudence.

886. ENVY

Those who don't know history are sometimes envious of those who do.

887. ESSENTIALS

It is accurate to say, "We are not in collusion with Rome and its shenanigans, but we are in communion with the Vatican II Catholic essentials of the faith."

888. CLARIFICATION

Roman Catholicism desperately needs to clearly distinguish between its discipline and its doctrine if ecumenism is to be fruitful.

889. INDULGENCES

The only indulgences some know are chocolate.

890. **DEMURE**

It's a sad day when one's beauty is taken for granted.

891. **EMERGENCY RESPONDER**

When suffering, disappointments, and trials don't make us more compassionate, then it's time to call in a Prayer Practitioner or a Meditative Man.

892. **TWOSOME**

Hope and Perseverance make a grand couple.

893. **NOT COINCIDENTAL**

Have you ever taken off your bathrobe, knocked your glasses out of your pajama shirt pocket, and had them land, not on the hard tile floor, but safely (lens upward) on the soft inner sole of your spouse's right shoe?

894. **PAYBACK**

He who insults G-d insults me. One big difference: G-d is much more patient.

895. **THINK TWICE**

Who is not leery of anyone who belittles blessings?

896. **VIEWPOINT**
What many consider a problem, others consider a privilege.

897. **LOFTIER**
A solitary rose of consolation while one is alive is better than a bouquet of orchids when one is dead.

898. **UPLIFT**
Nothing brightens up and aromatizes the house more than brewing a fresh pot of three blends of coffee: Chock full o'Nuts, Bustelo, Green Mountain Coffee, a little more Chock full o'Nuts, and a stick of cinnamon.

899. **DISCOVERY**
Some discover their sexuality in private; others in and through the media.

900. **IMPLANTED CELL PHONE**
A cell phone is not imbedded in the skin; therefore, it cannot be answered immediately—much less, when one is in the shower.

901. **WOW!**
If fifty billion brain cells are within the human cranium, and at least a century will be needed to map the brain, then at least 1,369,863 brain cells will have to be mapped each day.

902. **HAVE/HAVE NOT**
You either have it or you don't—applicable to valor, values, and money.

903. **QUANDARY**
How could one answer the e-mail of a man's wife and not address the husband? Little did one know the husband's name was Carol.

904. **POSITIVE/NEGATIVE**
For some, lovemaking, foreplay, and genital arousal are merely mutual masturbatory maneuvers.

905. **TRIPLE TRIPODS**
Sincerity, serenity, simplicity
Moderation, balance, equanimity
Analysis, critique, discernment

906. JUDGMENT

One can't judge the world; how can one judge anyone?

907. WEALTH

Beauty, riches, and values are to be found in the most unexpected places.

908. WHAT?

Methane gas under immense pressure yields diamonds.

909. PONTIFEX MAXIMUS

Let each be a pontifex maximus, a great bridge builder, among, for, and with the people.

910. DILEMMA

Is it better to be respected and seemingly lose an argument, or win an argument but risk disunity?

911. PERSPECTIVE

What is beauty and art for some is pornography for others.

912. **NONSENSE**

Glorified nonsense under all its trappings is still nonsense.

913. **ADMIRABLE**

Financially poor are some but they are rich in faith and mental capacity.

914. **COLLEGIALITY**

Collegiality means care, contemplation, cooperation, and communication.

915. **SYCOPHANCY**

Sycophants sicken society by their excessively white sugar sweet sauce sayings.

916. **MEANINGLESS VOTE**

To a dictator, voting is meaningless.

917. **EVIL**

Once evil is done, it must perpetuate itself or succumb to truth.

918. **INCLUSION**

The Church includes more than just Christians.

919. **COLLEGIALITY/COMMUNAL COOPERATION**

Collegiality implies accountability, teamwork, community, prayer, the earnest desire to fulfill G-d's Will, openness, and respect. If any of the seven is missing, collegiality is weakened or destroyed.

920. **GOOD/BETTER . . .**

It is better to talk to, and best to talk with, than talk about someone.

921. **GIFT**

To turn seriousness into comedy is no small feat.

922. **REQUISITE**

To get into/unto the same emotional wavelength of someone without getting overly involved requires openness, sensitivity, research, and prayer.

923. **DUO**

Emotion influences the brain and the brain reinforces the emotions.

924. **PARADOX POSSIBILITIES**

Creative laughter can come from serious situations.

925. **UNEXPECTED BLESSINGS**

Making someone smile brings blessings upon you.

926. **HIGH BLOOD PRESSURE**

Being overly serious is like having a super supply of sodium in your system.

927. **GOVERNANCE**

Three ways to govern exist:

Autocracy—One rules and the rest obey.

Majority rule—Division, disunity, and discontentment can and will arise.

Unanimity—This must have the groundwork of goodwill, contemplation, community, collegiality, and cooperation.

928. **UNITY'S CHALLENGE**

Unity, like reform, takes a lot of work, heartache, disappointment, prayer, and creativity.

929. ANTICOLLEGIALITY

When you treat your brothers and sisters like sub-ordinates, volcanic disagreements are only a breath away.

930. PROTECTIVE VEST

Wisdom is a shield against ignorance, arrogance, avarice, and vice.

931. FASCINATION

The intricacies of electricity are capable of titillation, elevation, fascination, and shock.

932. BENEDICTIONS

To be responsible, respectful, reverent, and resourceful is to enjoy beautiful, bountiful blessings.

933. SMILE

A sincere smile bespeaks simplicity, approval, insight, and interest.

934. DEROGATION

If derogatory remarks are not acknowledged, much less recognized by the user, then uncouthness is ingrained in him.

935. CROZIER/SHEPHERD'S STAFF

A crozier not made of precious gold, nor of the toughest steel, but of rosewood and mahogany, is a very strong reminder of Vatican II in Progress.

936. BYPRODUCT

Words without weight follow when action, prayer, and study are missing.

937. EQUILIBRIUM

A delicate balance exists between emotional growth and intellectual progress.

938. VERSUS

What is called "culture" would be better termed "degeneration."

939. EAST/WEST #1

Out West, even small population states have big highway signs. In the East, big population states have small signs.

940. EAST/WEST #2

Out West, you say to a stranger, "Hello," and you get one in return. In the East, you say to a stranger, "Good morning," and you get a stare, a grunt, and folks wonder what you're up to.

941. MISLEADING TERM

To perpetuate lies is hardly divine inspiration, but rather diabolical daring.

942. MEMORY

What is mere memory for some is reinvigorating reality for others.

943. CONNIVANCE

Regardless of how it is used or abused, connivance is still connivance.

944. UNNECESSARY PERMISSION

To do good, one does not need permission.

945. SAINTS UNRECOGNIZED

In our own family, among our own relatives, friends, and even among strangers are Saints who are unrecognized.

946. **ADAPTABLE BURKA**

Whose wife uses an adaptable burka, a pant-skirt four inches below the knee, and has not gotten used to covering her head except in extremely cold, windy, and hot weather?

947. **RIDE**

Has anyone ever ridden his Yamaha with his yarmulke?

948. **STANDING**

Deeds determine a dame and a don.

949. **ASSESSMENT**

To some, history is a mere memory. For others, the past is a Present, Momentous Reality.

950. **ZENITH**

Truth trumps triumph.

951. **EMPATHY**

How does one enter into another's emotions without being overcome by them?

952. **ADO, ADO**

To make a big bustle about dues is like saying the Sunday collection is the most important part of the religious service.

953. **LIKE!**

Who doesn't like her coffee like her poetry—hot!

954. **PREPARATION**

Isn't the best preparation for an important project to thank G-d for the opportunity to begin?

955. **THANKS**

Gratitude implies a request for present and future assistance.

956. **MIXED UP**

If some folks were as good at communicating as they are about excommunicating, what a pleasantly peaceful place this would be.

957. **INHUMANE**

When one religious hierarch excommunicates one of his or her members for joining another religion, then ecumenism is mocked, belittled, and berated.

958. **PURIFICATION**

One's motives are purified the more one seeks Divine Guidance.

959. **MESSAGE**

Even when one is interrupted, there is a message from G-d.

960. **SMALL/BIG**

One continues to firmly believe that one's small, sincere prayers contribute to the solution of big world problems.

961. **SURNAME**

Bank$, the IR$, and multinational corporation$ all have the same last name—money.

962. **HEAVEN**

Celestial Happiness is a Matter of Degree, Intensity, and Personalization.

963. **OFFICE**

To be a president is to be elected; to be a grand inquisitor is to be selected.

964. HIDDEN

Interruptions, like interpretations, hide blessings.

965. PROPHETESS

One's needs must heed the admonitions of a prophetess.

966. SHIELD

Perseverance in Prayer is the Protective Shield, the Impenetrable Vest, against the onslaughts of bad news and evil influences.

967. PRIVILEGE

To concentrate two hours or more is a Blessing, a Privilege, and an Opportunity.

968. TEMPO

Maintaining a certain rhythm is the best way to tackle a task.

969. NUCLEAR WASTE

There must be a way of converting nuclear waste into clean, safe, and efficient energy.

970. **TENDENCY**

We constantly and creatively advance, or we contribute little or nothing to society.

971. **COMPANIONS**

With Brothers Air and Sun and Sister Soil, we are never alone.

972. **CREATIVE IDENTITY**

Our inner and outer realization and that of the universe(s) are creatively identical.

973. **POWERFUL POET**

Our Most Powerful Poet, the Poet of all poets, is None Other.

974. **SPECIALTY**

Succinct one-liners are the specialty of some.

975. **POPCORN**

No two kernels of popcorn pop alike.

976. **FLU**

The jungle crud is the flu with its continual flow of phlegm.

977. **SUBLIMATION**

The most sublime of matters must at times take second place to physical necessities.

978. **DISCRETION**

Discreet openness is an inspiration, an exquisite gift, and a blessing from G-d.

979. **CREDIT DUE**

Deeds, not an institution, declare a saint or a scoundrel.

980. **CAP BACKWARDS**

Youth and older men who wear their caps backwards must have supersensitive skin on the back of their necks that needs protection from the rays of the sun.

981. **AUTONOMY**

Freedom must never be renounced, rejected, nor repudiated.

982. **ONE AND THE SAME**

The blueprint of the Church must become the blueprint of collegiality.

983. **THREE IN ONE**

Adoration, adulation, and worship are triplets that the Angels and the Saints offer to G-d.

984. **ANTECEDENCE**

"Our" takes precedence over "I."

985. **COMMON KNOWLEDGE**

Soon secrets will no longer be secrets.

986. **IGNORANCE**

. . . knows no limits.

987. **ACHIEVEMENT**

More is accomplished by completing little tasks well than by tackling a big job in one full swoop.

988. **SACRILEGE**

If some acts are considered sacrilegious, what can be said of atrocities far worse than sacrilege?

989. **A SCOLDING**

A bawling-out is a love call in a high-pitched voice with extremely high volume.

990. **COMMON GOOD**

Some have about as much appreciation for the common good as a coiled up cobra ready to strike a meandering, measly mouse.

991. **BOLEADORAS**

Fear, trepidation, and timidity are *boleadoras* (the leather balls on a gaucho's rope) that impede our progress.

992. **SORROWFUL SISTERS**

Grief, sadness, and lamentation tear at the heart and leave one almost "soulless."

993. **UNIVERSAL GOOD**

What is good for everyone is good for the individual.

994. **TWO-WAY STREET**

Respect is a two-way street. As one gives, so one receives.

995. **PUT UP OR . . .**

If one can make an opus or situation better but doesn't, then one shouldn't bewail, bemoan, complain, and criticize.

996. **TEMPORARY/PERMANENT**

Do not confuse a temporary title with a permanent position.

997. **QUALITY**

What a difference exists between solid historical content and mere sales pitch or emotional fervor.

998. **SUBSTITUTE**

If television is lacking, turn on your imagination.

999. **NOW**

Often, time is not what we save but what we enjoy.

1000. **REVENGE**

Negligence is a form of revenge.

1001. VARIANCE

Leadership and dominance differ, as do justice and tyranny.

1002. BEST

To do one's best is not an option but an order, a divine mandate, in one's best interest.

1003. APPRECIATION

Giving thanks must always precede petition.

1004. FLAWLESSNESS

Certain people hate to admit they make mistakes.

1005. COMPLEMENTARY?

Being well read does not mean being well accomplished.

1006. WONDER WORD

The Wonder Word of all wonder words is G-d.

1007. PERCEPTIVENESS

Vain competition exists in the eye of the beholder, and so does abuse of authority. One cannot address one without addressing the other. Until this happens, justice remains gagged and progress stymied.

1008. HISTORY

. . . is what it is and not what others would like it to be.

1009. OVERSIGHT

Some are so up to date on the latest news but aren't up to date on the Newest News.

1010. REASSESS

Those who cry out, "Slander, calumny, libel!" should check their facts as well as their emotions.

1011. CONTRAST

The human body is most beautiful, marvelous in life and most grotesque in death.

1012. ENCOMPASSING

Love reveals, seals, and satisfies.

1013. LOVE'S LAW

Slowly one begins to understand, appreciate, and fulfill Love's Law.

1014. TOUCH

One touches, but many sensations escape one's sense.

1015. TEARS

. . . soften and harden death's pain of separation.

1016. CATHARS

Some have as much appreciation for the Cathars and their history as can fit in a thimble or cover a thumbnail.

1017. FINESSE

Managers need to maintain the finishing touch of finesse if they are to remain top-notch in their field.

1018. SLEEP FAST

Fasting from sleep ranks among the greatest, and most meritorious, penances of all time.

1019. **WATCH OUT**

Flattery comes before force.

1020. **OPEN**

We may be ornery, bad tempered, crabby, and cantankerous, but we are open, honest, sincere, and aboveboard.

1021. **ADMISSION**

How hard it is for those in authority to admit they are wrong.

1022. **DISSIMILARITY**

The poor and the sick can offer the richest, most powerful prayers, while the rich and healthy can have the poorest and weakest of prayers.

1023. **FIGHT**

Some fight to hide their wrongs. Others fight for principle.

1024. FLAGELLATION OR . . .

Rather than using nightly flagellation and a crown of metal points to control the desires of the flesh, certain individuals would have been better off to simply masturbate or, better yet, get married.

1025. PRICE

When one sticks out one's neck for principle, one must be on the lookout for the proverbial head chopper.

1026. INVENTIVENESS

Simple suggestions often lead to incredible challenges.

1027. INDECISIVE

Sometimes we don't know when selfishness ends and prudence begins.

1028. LANGUAGE

Every sound has its code and language.

1029. TERRIBLE TRIPLETS: H. I. G.

Hypocrisy, injustice, and greed weigh heavily on the world's woes.

1030. **BLANK CHECK**

Religion must never become a blank check for evildoing.

1031. **WILD GOOD**

Good spreads like Wild Fire.

1032. **TWINS**

Gratitude and thankfulness are identical twins born of a dedicated heart.

1033. **STALWARTS**

Often the "rejects" of one organization become the stalwarts and supporters of another.

1034. **INSCRUTABLE**

Truth cannot be put into a box, nor adequately explained, elucidated, or expounded, but only pointed to.

1035. **CREATIVITY'S BOUNTY**

Multitudinous possibilities spring, bounce, and pounce from every creative act.

1036. SHOCKER

Those who think they are infallibly educated are in for a surprise.

1037. FRAUD AND TREACHERY

To impose a law without adequate explanation and without the consent of the governed is fraudulent and treacherous.

1038. DIFFICULT PEOPLE

Those who don't deal with difficult people don't deal with themselves, either.

1039. SURPRISE

Out of every difficulty and adversity is born a new opportunity for creativity and inventiveness.

1040. BE CAUTIOUS

Those who work for reform must be wary lest they become powermongers themselves.

1041. TONALITY

Some voices lull one to sleep; others spur and inspire one to action, while others convey condescension, overbearing authority, and superiority.

1042. **ASTONISHMENT**

To turn life's ordinary events into proverbs is an undoubtedly delightful surprise.

1043. **TWO MOST BEAUTIFUL**

The two most beautiful words in the five thousand–plus languages of the world, not counting the dialects, are "Thank you."

1044. **GROUNDWORK**

Everything one has done before was in preparation for what one is doing now.

1045. **ORGANIZATION**

. . . is nothing more than dividing and subdividing, giving assignments, checking and rechecking details, and adding or subtracting details.

1046. **AMAZING**

Billions of years old are the rays of the sun by the time they reach our Earth.

1047. **INNOCENCE**

The innocence of a child is entrancing, enthralling, enchanting, and powerful.

1048. ONE OF BILLIONS

. . . of stars is the sun.

1049. HOP, SKIP, JUMP

Ninety-three million miles away is the sun.

1050. POSSESSIVE POSSESSION

What good is it to possess all the truth if *all the truth* does not possess us?

1051. STRANGE GALAXY MYSTERY

Strange stars are magnetars.

1052. PULSARS

. . . emit less energy than magnetars.

1053. TWIN SPOUSES

Science and religion are twin spouses—one nourishes and nurtures the mind; the other saturates, stimulates, and stirs the soul.

1054. JUDICIOUSNESS

Thinking through before speaking and acting on important matters is shrewd, discreet, prudent.

1055. THIMBLEFUL

Some have as much prudence as can fit in a capsule of medicine.

1056. TWO SIDES

What appears for some as mere politics is a matter of justice for others.

1057. RESPECTABLE

Some become "respectable" by the force of the sword, the might of money, and the weight and influence of time.

1058. MISPLACED

Better adorn with precious gems the neck of thy rotting woman's corpse than live a life of piety, while thy son unattended be.

1059. HIDDEN KEYS

To discover and develop the hidden talents of prisoners and convicts are boons and benefits to society.

1060. TOO BAD

Those who love praise and adulation but hate those who disagree with them are sorry loser leaders.

1061. **WHICH POWER?**

Which do we choose: the power of money, the power of the pen, the power of prayer, or none of the above?

1062. **MARVELOUS MIX**

Sadness is bitter; however, sadness with humor and wit is a marvelous mix.

1063. **JUSTICE, JUSTICE**

To speak of justice and evenhandedness in some sectors is like adding oil to fire.

1064. **METRONOME**

A flickering flame keeps time with any tune.

1065. **MANTRA MADNESS**

Religiously, rogues rant against and ravage their rivals.

1066. **BROTHER BIRDS**

The black beaks of my brother birds break up hard bits of corn bread and bring delight to my being.

1067. **OR ELSE**

One must continually practice standing and sitting up straight or become stoop-shouldered.

1068. **DECISION**

To lose or to choose a challenge lies within the competence, capacity, and capability of each.

1069. **CLASS**

There exist the stingy rich, the generous, philanthropic rich, the dirty/filthy rich, and the clean rich.

1070. **CATHOLICS**

There exist Catholics, Roman Catholics, Opus Dei Catholics, and Vatican II Catholics.

1071. **DICTATOR**

Whether one be religious or not, a dictator is still a despot.

1072. **CREATIVE TIME**

A creative work can take nine minutes, nine hours, nine days, nine months, or more.

1073. **TRANSFORMATIVE**

To make beauty out of tragedy and misfortune is a bountiful blessing.

1074. **POSITIVE**

To see a privilege rather than a problem is powerfully perceptive.

1075. **INGENUITY**

Imagination, willingness, and openness are the tripods of creativity.

1076. **ALIENS**

Are aliens really aliens or angels in visible forms?

1077. **CULTURE**

. . . is the college and the caring crown of a people.

1078. **JEWEL**

Generosity shines like a precious jewel amidst the rocks and dirt of the world.

1079. **UNWELCOME MAT**

The "unwelcome mat" for today's prophet involves getting cut off from the defense of one's own name, character, innovation, creativity, and constructive criticism.

1080. **CONFUSION**

Some confuse collegiality with dictatorship—with or without religious robes.

1081. **MEMOIR**

History ought to be the text and context of our lives.

1082. **MALICE'S X**

He who is rude, crude, obnoxious, and dictatorial with a few loyal colleagues and brothers will inevitably conduct himself in similar fashion with others, too.

1083. **BELATED THANKS**

We take for granted the simple yet necessary functions until we are unable to do them.

1084. DO & DONE BY

Those who cast dirt on others will be buried by it before their time.

1085. TRIPLE MARK

Whoever carries a grudge is cold, callous, and calculating.

1086. OPINION

One's own opinion, bloated with pride and near-sighted, needs outside bifocal objectivity.

1087. PREVARICATION

Lies added to lies and multiplied by lies still equal lies.

1088. COMPARISON

Some are better writers than speakers.

1089. DISGRACE

Corruption and falsehood shame one's name.

1090. SILENCE'S SIN

Some sully their souls by their silence. Betrayal of their brothers belies their feigned innocence.

1091. **SIMONIAC**
Those who pawn off piety in exchange for phony-colored gold coins are sellers of the sacred.

1092. **MISNOMER**
What some call ecumenism should more aptly be called contrived monopoly.

1093. **INCOMPARABLE**
Nothing nurtures more than Nature.

1094. **TRUTH'S INTRANSIENCE**
Neither the strength nor the height of injustice can extinguish Truth's Light.

1095. **ALEXANDR SOLZHENITSYN**
Solzhenitsyn shakes up our synapses, our collective conscience, and succors us.

1096. **MISINFORMATION**
. . . wins the day when one fails to tell the truth.

1097. **LUCIDITY?**
Let's not confuse and confound fatigue with defeat.

1098. NEUROTIC MONSTER

Foot-dragging, criticism, and negativity construct a triple-headed monster.

1099. CURE

The venom of others can be our antidote if we learn to handle it properly.

1100. HATRED

. . . is worse than an eastern diamondback rattlesnake's bite.

1101. ACCOLADES

Those who yearn for accolades must earn them. Rank, position, and title do not guarantee honors, praise or tributes.

1102. VIPER

An injustice cannot remain simply an "internal" matter for long. Sooner or later, its ugly head will show itself for what it is.

1103. **SISTER AND BROTHER**

Worry and Wonder have the same parents. The first
frets, fritters, and gets nowhere. The second sees with
the eyes of the soul.

1104. **ROOT**

Professing piety does not do away with one's pernicious, profligate past.

1105. **AFTERMATH**

Extreme strictness leads to overindulgence.

1106. **SOCIAL DECORUM**

Some have decorum and dignity; some don't. Those
who don't, revile, insult, and scorn those who do.

1107. **STAY THE COURSE**

If you are right, stay the course. If not, you'll fall from
your horse.

1108. **ATTRACTION**

Where much money, power lie, there many gravitate
nearby.

1109. JUSTIFIABLE OUTCOME

May potent proverbs sear the souls of extremists, tyrants, and terrorists.

1110. EITHER

What one can't profess in prose, let one express in poetry or proverbs.

1111. PROVERB

A proverb, an inspiration, is like food a mother pelican gives its young.

1112. GREATER

Obedience may be greater than sacrifice, but charity still remains greater than obedience.

1113. CONTEMPLATIVE CONVERSATION

Some think they have to keep their conversation going even on the phone, and never allow for any silence so that what is said can sink in.

1114. PREJUDICE'S MIRROR

Those who suffer from prejudice can also be the perpetrators of prejudice.

1115. **TRUTH'S DEMANDS**

The pursuit of truth demands the flushing and fer-reting out of one's own prejudices, feelings, and tendencies.

1116. **EXTREME ADVERSARIALISM**

An entire community, a city, county, or state legal system can be guilty of extreme adversarialism.

1117. **TRUTH VS. FRIENDSHIP**

Friendship must never trump truth.

1118. **TRUTH'S MODUS PROCEDENDI**

Double-, triple-, quadruple-checking must be com-pleted if truth is to triumph.

1119. **UNIVERSAL LANGUAGE**

One need not be a linguist nor a polyglot to speak love's language.

1120. **ABOVE AND BEYOND**

Are there more synapses in one's brain than stars in a galaxy?

1121. CANDIDNESS

Open your heart and your mind. There true treasure you will find.

1122. HIGH CARD

Some prefer an institution of rigidity, rigor, regulations, and rules to one of care, concern, cooperation, and *caritas* (charity).

1123. AFFINITY

We are both benefactors and victims of technology.

1124. OUTDONE

Death denigrates, devastates, and destroys, but love destroys death.

1125. APPETITE

Love devours and engulfs death. The more we love, the more death is devoured and engulfed.

1126. SENSE

Sharp as a surgeon's scalpel is the sense of justice of a select few. Butter knife–dull is the sense of justice of others.

1127. **SIMPLE**

Sounds challenge the mightiest of men.

1128. **FREE PASS**

Perfection, like doing good, needs permission from
no one.

1129. **DAMS AND DIKES**

Certain institutions are like unnecessary dams and
dikes that hold back the waters of religious freedom.

1130. **LEGACY**

Even after death, detraction, defamation, and derision
will not demean the honest.

1131. **ANGLE**

Some are labeled too emotional and intense, while
others, who act the same way, are called energetic and
assertive.

1132. **INTRUSION**

By intrusive fax, too many merchants mark and mar-
ket their merchandise without our permission.

1133. **BLIND SPOTS**

Even efficiency has its blind spots and does not ensure success.

1134. **PSYCHO CHANGE**

If one is as friendly, affable, and congenial as a rattlesnake coiled and set to strike, then one needs a complete personality makeover.

1135. **STINGY**

A fair number of folks are not only stingy, tightfisted with their money, time, and talent, but also with their loyalty.

1136. **SOLUTIONS**

History can still provide solutions to present problems.

1137. **SPEECH**

What one's tongue doesn't utter, one's heart does.

1138. **TESTAMENT**

Prophetic witness, preaching, and teaching are intimately linked. One must, therefore, weigh one's words well.

1139. **MATURITY**

A crisis is a trial by fire of one's maturity and sensibleness.

1140. **EVIDENCE**

Let the facts of history prove a person a Saint, not the dastardly dictums of dictators.

1141. **MOTIVE**

To do good without applause has Holiness as its Cause.

1142. **REAP**

Bit by bit, our efforts shall reap a rich harvest.

1143. **WORD CONCENTRATION**

A proverb is a concentration of well-chosen words.

1144. **DEFAMATION OR?**

One's deeds defame or make one well known.

1145. **FLAWS**

Headstrong and selfish people are often uncouth, crude, and rude.

1146. **DISPOSITION**

Good news is ill received by those ill disposed.

1147. **ROMANISM'S BUG**

Too many reformists still have remnants of
Romanism in their system.

1148. **AWARE**

Certain folks should be ashamed of themselves;
however, shame is felt only by those who have a
conscience.

1149. **TWOFOLD PURPOSE**

A tallit serves a utilitarian as well as a prayerful
purpose.

1150. **SHARED INFALLIBILITY**

Like the pope, I, too, am infallible—sometimes.

1151. **PEDAGOGY**

Example ever remains the greatest teacher.

1152. **TOIL BEFORE TREASURE**

For most of us, the goal comes before the gold thread.

1153. **MEAN MEASURE**

To the grumpy, everyone else is disagreeable, disconcerting, and displeasing.

1154. **HIGHER CALLING**

A baby can make a man; study, prayer, appropriate action, and sickness stabilize a saint.

1155. **LASTING LEGACY**

When testimonials are beacons of hope in our turbulent times, and inspiration for the downtrodden, then they are lasting legacies of love.

1156. **INFECTIVITY**

Keeping the thorn of hate in one's heart hurts not only oneself but others, too.

1157. **TWIN**

Pelagianism is vowed celibacy's twin.

1158. **VIOLATOR**

To violate the Seal of Confession is dastardly, damnable, and deserving of derision.

1159. CALLS

Prayer and study are calls to action.

1160. TALENT

Concentration is a great gift. When it is broken, one feels incomplete.

1161. RESULT

If a child makes a man, what can be said of a celibate?

1162. DEVIATIONS

To be arrogant is displeasing and dishonest. To be arrogant and ignorant is a double disgrace.

1163. UNFIT

A warped character is worse than having holes in one's clothes.

1164. WRONGDOING

Crime has its own punishment.

1165. RUSE

Many can look good on the outside but be dangerously ill on the inside.

1166. VALOR

. . . has no age limit.

1167. FRIENDSHIP

To my friends, my hand in friendship; to the rest, the scalpel of reserve.

1168. GREED'S OFFSPRING

The vow of poverty does not protect one from avarice.

1169. VERBAL VAMPIRES

Those who backbite and those who listen to such trashy talk but don't defend the victim(s) are verbal vampires.

1170. RECOMMENDATIONS?

Ecclesial officials' recommendations of sexually abusive priests is like the fox's testimony that the blood-smeared mouth of the coyote is proof of his inalienable defense of the helpless chickens.
(See http://catholics4change.com/2012/03/20/
the-list-cardinal-bevilacqua-didnt-want-you-to-see/)

1171. SCARRED MEMORY

Vestiges of the Inquisition still remain, silhouetting our present memory.

1172. DEVIATION

The Curia—papism par excellence, power, politics, pressure, persecution. Monopoly, yes; institution, yes; church, no.

1173. DISGUISE

Ferguson, Missouri, has shown the world the ugly face of prejudice.

1174. MIDDLE WAY?

Is there anything grand about the grand jury of Ferguson, Missouri?

1175. BULLY

A strong white minority pushes around a black majority or vice versa.

1176. RECOMPENSE

The more the powers that be backbite, defame, ridicule, and slander us, the more we pray for them and for our weakest members.

1177. **EVENTS**

One should contemplate history as present events.

1178. **WORD**

Of all the trillions and trillions to the nth power of words in five thousand–plus languages that exist on planet Earth, *one* word stands out among all the others.

1179. **BEYOND BELIEF**

The universe(s) is/are one trillionth of a trillionth of a trillionth of a second old. If something had no mass, would it move faster than the speed of light? Is matter Concentrated Energy? Are matter and energy the same?

1180. **VERIFICATION**

Truth tells the tale.

1181. **UNPREDICTABLE**

When matter and antimatter collide, Who knows what happens?

1182. COMPASSION

Don't worry about what you will say or how you will say it. Let your eyes and your heart be the spokesmen of your sympathy.

1183. POWERS OF SILENCE

Silence, like a surgeon's scalpel, incises excess, brings healing to society, and submerges the soul in the sublimity of the Supreme Self.

1184. PROBE

Proverbs, like science, probe truth's profundity.

1185. S. S. S.

In Silence and Simplicity, one reaches Significance.

1186. FINE TAPESTRY

Poetry is a finely woven tapestry of words.

1187. POEM'S PURPOSE

Powerful poems penetrate the periphery of personality.

1188. **THREE R'S**

Poetry has Rhyme, Rhythm, and Rationale.

1189. **PARTIALITY**

If Rome has all the truth, the whole bloody truth, then why does it reveal only some of it?

1190. **EMOTION**

"Feeling is the heart of thought and the life of poetry." (Will & Ariel Durant, *The Age of Voltaire*, p. 40)

1191. **PRECIOUS STONE**

A proverb written down is an emerald in one's crown.

1192. **SCAM**

Signing a forced confession is like signing a laicization document. Both involve signing to a lie.

1193. **SHOAH (SHAME)**

Some teach ethics: cover up evil, avoid scandal, silence victims, excommunicate protesters.

1194. ENDOWMENT

To have a powerful, prayerful imagination is a grand gift.

1195. PORNOGRAPHY

Is pornography a form of safe sex?

1196. FIVE AND TWENTY

Never buy a paper shredder that has the instructions "Run for five minutes and let it cool for twenty minutes." Efficiency—so-so.

1197. CORPORATE GREED

When financial gain supercedes the well-being of others, disrupts the environment as does fracking, and even unduly influences legislators, then mass protest is in order.

1198. PANTOMINE OF THE PROMINENT

There are those who hide behind their display of exquisitely expensive works of art, who glory in having billionaires in their club, but who do little or nothing to improve society.

1199. **D3**

Like the rays of the sun, dynamic, vigorous, and vital
is G-d.

1200. **RELATIVE?**

Is an in-law related to an outlaw?

1201. **CRITERIA**

Sometimes our standards for Sainthood are stricter
than G-d's.

1202. **WEARIED WORKER**

Let weariness awaken in us the Superbly Gallant
Strength of our G-d..

1203. **MISSION**

Far from men's eyes, one does daring deeds.

1204. **MITE**

"The widow's mite" has more might than the mighty's
money.

1205. **HEROISM**

Feeling fear in its intense variant forms and conquering that trepidation is heroism.

1206. **EASIER**

For some, it is easier to treat with contempt, to criticize, and to condemn rather than to console, counsel, and comfort.

1207. **HEAT**

Many people must have excessive heat emanating from their heads because even in the dead of winter, they wear no head covering.

1208. **CAPTIVITY**

Some are held captive by their capricious whims, unruly understanding, sudden sickness, or perpetual prejudice, still others by their multiple obligations.

1209. **COMMITMENT**

Some take the vow of poverty while others live by its Spirit.

1210. **BUILDING COMMUNITY**

To build community, all involved must embrace collegiality, devote themselves to prayer, and be open to the promptings of the Spirit and to the promptings of their colleagues.

1211. **LIVED COLLEGIALITY**

Collegiality must be lived and not just taught and talked about.

1212. **CONDITIONAL OBEDIENCE**

Spousal obedience should always live the condition "If you are right."

1213. **OPUS**

One's work can be musical, meaningful, beautiful, and insightful. Or it can be like its author: sour, dour, and severe.

1214. **NUPTIALS**

Heaven and earth are united in beautiful harmony.

1215. **COMMUNIST NUN**

Is a Communist nun a Comrade Sister?

CHAPTER ELEVEN

SONGS/MUSIC

1216. **PRECIOUS, PRECIOSO**
(to the tune of "O, G-d of Loveliness")

English:
Brilliant are YOU, O LORD.
Steady are YOU, O LORD.
Worthy of LOVE, my LORD.
Precious are YOU, my LORD.

Spanish:
Brillante, mi Señor.
Firmeza, mi Señor.
Amoroso, Señor.
Precioso, mi Señor.

Hebrew:
Ya-kir Gadol, Yahweh.
Ah-tzir Gadol, Yahweh.
Yah-kir Gadol, Yahweh.
Yeh-re-heh ya-kar, Yahweh.
(Repeat four times)

Arabic:
/Kool/ /Ja/-/mil/ /hah/- /noon/ /Al/-/lah)
(Repeat four times)

1217. HANDEL AND BACH

"George Friedrich Handel wedded Italian melody to German counterpoint, and Johann Sebastian Bach was the completion and perfection of the polyphonic, fugal, contrapuntal past."
(Will & Ariel Durant, *The Age of Voltaire*, p. 42)

1218. BEETHOVEN AND GOYA

Ludwig van Beethoven and Francisco Goya both became deaf, but complemented each other in music and art.

1219. MUSIC'S TRICK

Joseph Louis Lagrange "learned to like music . . . which is a trick that mathematics plays upon the ear . . . because 'it isolates me. I hear the first three measures; the fourth I distinguish nothing; I give myself up to my thoughts; nothing interrupts me; and it is thus that I solve more than one difficult problem.'"
(Will & Ariel Durant, *The Age of Voltaire*, p. 513, in E. T. Bell, *Men of Mathematics*, p. 17)

1220. AN ECUMENICAL FORM

Music is one of the true ecumenical forms.

1221. **ARTS**

Out of difficulties, distress, duress, and disappointment are born proverbs, poems, prose, songs, and art.

1222. **ARTISTE MUSICALE MAGNIFIQUE**

G-d sang us into existence with music tingling our toes, harmonizing our hair, and bouncing off our bones.

1223. **MUSIC ME**

When the Lord made me, He or She put music in my hair, rhythm in my toes, and syncopation in my bones.

1224. **BASS**

In too many bands and recordings, the bass overwhelms, overextends, and overpowers the melody and the lyrics.

1225. **PRIMARY CAUSE**

G-d is the Cause of the new and old songs one sings.

1226. **ONE IN THREE**

Music, Melody, and Superb Song of Songs is G-d.

1227. SINGER

We must let the Lord sing new songs through us.

1228. MUSIC MARVELOUS

The Most Marvelous Music is G-d.

1229. COUNTERPOINT

Beautiful music is the counterpoint to sadness, tragedy, fear, and lethargy.

CHAPTER TWELVE

WRITING

1230. LIFELESS LITERATURE

. . . may be grammatically correct, but dry, languid, and practically lifeless.

1231. SAGACITY

To choose one's words well is wisdom.

1232. ARMAMENTS

Our pens and computers are our slingshots. Truth is our stone, a hundred times stronger than the strongest steel.

1233. TWIN BIRTHS

Out of pain, grief, joy, and openness, prose and poetry are born.

1234. INTOLERANCE

If we are prejudiced against someone or something, the substance of our writing, speech, and actions will reflect that intolerance.

1235. DRAINED BUT REFRESHED

Writing exhausts and refreshes an author.

1236. INSIGHT

Weigh your words carefully lest they become pro-phetically true.

1237. MYSTIC

The prophetess cannot always weigh her words nor her actions well because they are not always her own.

1238. EXPOSÉ

Writing reveals the author's soul.

1239. THERAPY

Writing soothes frustration and assuages anger.

1240. DIARY

A checkbook is a minifinancial journal.

1241. WEIGH

Let us weigh our words wisely. Verbiage is dead weight.

1242. **VERBIAGE GARBAGE**

Thoughtlessly, carelessly, recklessly, and disgustingly written material is not worth the paper it is written on.

1243. **MAXIMS**

Writing proverbs teaches one to look to, to be more open to, and to depend more on G-d.

1244. **FROM SCRATCH**

Writing your life's story is like building your own log home from scratch.

1245. **APPLE PIE**

Writing a proverb is like baking a delicious home-baked pie: washed, peeled, and cut green apples, brown sugar, locally grown honey, cinnamon powder, a pinch of salt, and tenderness.

1246. **REFINEMENT**

Editing is the fine grooming of language.

1247. AUTOBIOGRAPHY

Removing writer's block and being more objective can both be achieved by writing one's autobiography in the third person singular and writing as fast as one can.

1248. FIRST DRAFT

Writing a first draft is like digging out the foundation for a basement and putting in the footings of one's "home" autobiography.

1249. WORDSMITH

To make sentences as pleasurable as possible is to begin a wordsmith's craft.

1250. SHARPNESS

Written words, sharper than a surgeon's scalpel, cut clean, quickly, keenly.

1251. DETERMINED WRITER

Despite a slow, steady step, a certain friend has a determined spirit.

1252. COMPOSITION

Every grand opus begins with a well-written word.

1253. LIFE ENCLOSED

I live in a wondrous womb world of words. Writing wrings out the best of me.

1254. ADVOCATES

To help with writing, call upon the Archangel Uriel, Thomas Aquinas, Shakespeare, Alexander Pope, Jacques Voltaire, Victor Hugo, Benjamin Franklin, Samuel Clemens, Ernest Hemingway, and the Nobel Prize Winners of Literature.

1255. GUESS

What is material but brings about a nonmaterial entity? Answer: written words, which convey an idea or ideas.

1256. RETOOL

Sharpen your words when they are dull, soften them when they are harsh, and embolden them when they are weak.

1257. PROPHETIC LITERATURE

Great literature is prophetic. It upsets, engages, and challenges.

1258. WORDS

. . . sing, sting, sag, or brag.

1259. YELLOW JOURNALISTS

Some journalists have as much finesse with their interviewees as a vicious viper with its prey.

1260. EXCURSION

One is on a verbal journey through Shakespeare. Each page read aloud is a marvelous mile of splendid sound and sense. Only 712 miles remain.

1261. SUPERB SHAKESPEARE

The rhythm, rhyme, symmetry, sound, and wisdom of Shakespeare are pleasing to the ear and challenging to the brain.

1262. ENDEAVOR

What Michelangelo carved out of marble, one must carefully craft with one's words.

1263. TOOLS

One's slab of marble is one's ream of paper. One's hammer, chisel, point, and roundel are one's pad, pen, pencil, and computer/typewriter.

1264. MASTERPIECE

Our David marble masterpiece will be our life's story.

1265. ICON

The sounds and substance of Shakespeare silhouette the world's soul.

1266. CALLING

The philosopher, the poet, and the wordsmith have the will to weave words of wisdom into a tough tapestry of tenderness.

1267. SCRIPT SANCTUARY

In writing, we find refuge.

1268. VISIONARY

Dare to say, to write when research proves you right. Fear not reproach, reprimand, pain, nor slight.

1269. SPURTS AND STARTS

In spurts and starts, we write. Our spurts surprise us and our starts startle us. When we can write for ten hours straight, we are even more astonished.

1270. DICHOTOMY

Writing wrests the best and the worst from us.

1271. REVISION

Revising one's writing is like replacing old panels with new gesture design ones.

1272. WINDOWS

Clear writing is the spotless window of writing.

1273. FRAMEWORK

A first draft is like an architect's blueprint—detailed and precise.

1274. ENHANCEMENT

Reading is an encouragement, a boost, a shot in the arm, to writing.

1275. RIVETS

Periods are the rivets, press studs, and fasteners of a row of words with their corresponding numbers. Periods are the rivets of writing.

BIBLIOGRAPHY

"700 New Synapses Every Single Second." The Raising
     of America. http://www.raisingofamerica.
     org/700-new-synapses-every-single-second.

"A Brief History of Celibacy in the Catholic Church."
     FutureChurch. http://futurechurch.org/
     brief-history-of-celibacy-in-catholic-church.

Allen, Jr., John L. "A Vatican Watershed in Transparency."
     National Catholic Reporter, August 3, 2012.

Berry, Jason. "Kung Still Resists the 'Roman Inquisition.'"
     National Catholic Reporter, December 6, 2012.

"Bible Gateway Passage: Genesis 2:15–3:21—New
     International Version." Bible Gateway. https://www.
     biblegateway.com/passage/?search=Genesis 2:15-3:21.

BishopAccountability.org–Documenting the Abuse Crisis in the Roman Catholic Church.

Bradford, Sarah. *Lucrezia Borgia: Life, Love and Death in Renaissance Italy.* New York: Penguin Books, 2004.

Cavendish, Richard. "Execution of Florentine Friar Savonarola." HistoryToday. http://www.historytoday.com/richard-cavendish/execution-florentine-friar-savonarola.

Cawthorne, Nigel. *Sex Lives of the Popes.* London: Carlton Pubishing Group, 2004.

Clarke, Kevin. "Pope Francis Is Not a Marxist, but Make No Mistake: He Will Challenge the World's Leading Capitalist Power." *Washington Post.* July 14, 2015. https://www.washingtonpost.com/news/acts-of-faith/wp/2015/07/14/pope-francis-is-not-a-marxist-but-make-no-mistake-he-will-challenge-the-worlds-leading-capitalist-power/.

Durant, Will, and Ariel Durant. *The Age of Voltaire.* New York: Simon and Schuster, 1965.

Eliot, Samuel. *The History of Liberty.* Vol. 2. Boston: Little, Brown, 1853.

Goldman, Bruce. "Stunning Details of Brain Connections Revealed." *Science Daily*. November 17, 2010. http://www.sciencedaily.com/releases/2010/11/101117121803.htm.

Matthews, Susan. "The List Cardinal Bevilacqua Didn't Want You to See." Catholics4Change. March 20, 2012. http://catholics4change.com/2012/03/20/the-list-cardinal-bevilacqua-didnt-want-you-to-see/.

Malone, Clare. "Holy Rollers, Nuns on the Bus." *Corpus Reports*, November 2013.

"Mao Tse Tung: Worst Hygiene in a Dictator." Democratic Underground Forums. http://www.democraticunderground.com/discuss/duboard.php?az=view_all&address=105x409054.

Moses, Paul. *The Saint and the Sultan*. New York: Doubleday Religion, 2009.

"Opium of the People." Wikipedia. http://en.wikipedia.org/wiki/Opium_of_the_people.

"Paul Allen Just Got One Step Closer to Mapping the Human Brain." *Forbes*. May 14, 2015. http://www.forbes.com/sites/arleneweintraub/2015/05/14/paul-allen-just-got-one-step-closer-to-mapping-the-human-brain.

Prose, Donald. "Science and Theology Meet Again." *Corpus Reports*, July 2010.

Sahtouris, Elisabet. "Towards a Future Global Science: Axioms for Modeling a Living Universe." *World Future Review*, 2009, 5-16.

Smith, Frank Thomas. "The Gnostic Gospels by Eileen Pagels." *Southern Cross Review*. http://southerncrossreview.org/2/gnostic.html.

"'Some Definite Service' by John Henry Cardinal Newman." Apple Seeds. http://www.appleseeds.org/Newman_My-Mission.htm.

"Vatican Official Warns of 'Dialogue of the Deaf' with LCWR." *National Catholic Reporter*. June 12, 2012. http://ncronline.org/blogs/ncr-today/vatican-official-warns-dialogue-deaf-lcwr.

Yallop, David. *The Power and the Glory: Inside the Dark Heart of John Paul II's Vatican.* New York: Carroll & Graf, 2007.

ACKNOWLEDGMENTS

Ilia G. Herrera: My "LuLu, Cucuroochu" is my inspiration, the sunshine of our home, and the refreshment of my years.

Special thanks are due to Christina Henry de Tessan, Andrea Dunlop, Kristin Mehus-Roe, Leslie Miller, Meghan Harvey, and Ben Grossblatt at Girl Friday Productions. Without their expertise, this book would not have been possible.

ABOUT THE AUTHOR

Patrick E. Trujillo, born in Mora, New Mexico, one of eight children, served as a Roman Catholic celibate priest for eighteen years in Wyoming, where he was director of Cursillos in Christianity, director of Spanish-Speaking Apostolate, and was a volunteer probation officer (juvenile division) for eight years in addition to his duties as pastor of the missions associated with his parishes.

In 1984, he married Ilia G. Herrera, who directed RENEW, a lay leadership development program in Spanish in the United States, and who had been imprisoned by the Cuban Communists in maximum security prisons from 1963 until 1973 for teaching religion to the poor as a Mystical Rose member of the Vanguards of Mary. She also spent two years under house arrest.

After moving to New Jersey, Trujillo worked as a bilingual academic counselor in Ossining Correctional Facility, formerly Sing-Sing Prison, for Mercy College, Tarrytown, New York.

Before retiring after twenty years of teaching, he became archbishop of the Archdiocese of Our Lady of Guadalupe of New Jersey, Inc., Old Catholic Church in America in 1999. Trujillo was consecrated a Roman Catholic bishop *"Sub-Conditione"* by Archbishop Emmanuel Milingo of Zambia, Africa. Milingo was consecrated a bishop by Pope Paul VI. Archbishop Trujillo has been the vice president of Married Priests Now! since 2004. In his spare time, he studies Hebrew and Arabic.

Made in the USA
San Bernardino, CA
04 January 2016